# LEAVING CERT

# LESS STRESS MORE SUCCESS

## English Revision
### Ordinary Level

Joseph Kelly

Gill & Macmillan

Gill & Macmillan
Hume Avenue
Park West
Dublin 12
with associated companies throughout the world
www.gillmacmillan.ie

© Joseph Kelly 2013

978 07171 5803 4
Design by Liz White Designs
Artwork by Derry Dillon
Print origination by Carole Lynch

*The paper used in this book is made from the wood pulp of managed forests. For every tree felled, at least one tree is planted, thereby renewing natural resources.*

All rights reserved.

No part of this publication may be copied, reproduced or transmitted in any form or by any means without written permission of the publishers or else under the terms of any licence permitting limited copying issued by the Irish Copyright Licensing Agency.

Any links to external websites should not be construed as an endorsement by Gill & Macmillan of the content or view of the linked material.

For permission to reproduce photographs, the author and publisher gratefully acknowledge the following:

© Alamy: 12, 13B, 27, 56, 59, 68C, 76, 84, 93; © Getty Images: 5, 11, 13TL, 13TR, 14, 25, 58, 68T, 73T, 73BL, 75L, 75C, 75R, 90T, 90B; © Rex Features: 10, 23, 73C, 73BR; Courtesy of Barry Ryan: 45; Courtesy of Google: 7; Courtesy of the State Examinations Commission: 1, 5, 31, 36, 37, 38.

The author and publisher have made every effort to trace all copyright holders, but if any has been inadvertently overlooked we would be pleased to make the necessary arrangement at the first opportunity.

# CONTENTS

● **Before the Exam**
  1. Exam Outline and Mental Preparation ..................................................1
  2. The Marking Scheme ...........................................................................6
  3. Language Genres in the Exam ............................................................12

● **Paper 1**
  4. Comprehension ...................................................................................15
  5. Composition ........................................................................................35

● **Paper 2**
  6. The Single Text ...................................................................................53
  7. The Comparative Study ......................................................................64
  8. Poetry ..................................................................................................73

● **Final Preparations for Exam Day**
  9. Time-keeping and Revision Checklist ................................................90
  10. Glossary of Useful Words ..................................................................94

## Acknowledgments

My sincere thanks to the boys and staff of Naas CBS, who helped with this book in many ways. I must also thank my wonderful parents, as well as my personal editor Emily-Anne. I hope this book helps in some way to improve the exam results of many hard-working students out there.

> This book is intended to bring confidence to all Leaving Certificate Ordinary Level students preparing for their English exam. With the right attitude and exam-focused knowledge, results will be maximised.

# Before the Exam

## 1 Exam Outline and Mental Preparation

- To understand the structure of the exam papers.
- To know the breakdown of marks allocated to each section of the course.
- To develop the right attitude to exam revision.
- To improve crucial reading skills.

There are special features throughout the book that are designed to make your revision easier. These include: aims, key points and exam focus notes. Each chapter begins with a list of **aims**: a broad statement of what you should expect to achieve in this chapter. **Key points** appear throughout and they serve as good reminders of essential information. **Exam focus** notes offer advice on getting the most out of your time during the exam.

## Structure of the exam

- Two papers.
- 200 marks each.
- 400 marks in total.

## Paper 1

Paper 1 has **two sections:**

---

2012. M.9

 **Coimisiún na Scrúduithe Stáit**
**State Examinations Commission**

LEAVING CERTIFICATE EXAMINATION, 2012

### English - Ordinary Level - Paper 1

Total Marks: 200

Wednesday, 6 June – Morning, 9.30 – 12.20

- This paper is divided into two sections,
  Section I COMPREHENDING and Section II COMPOSING.
- The paper contains **three** texts on the general theme of BEING A LEADER.
- Candidates should familiarise themselves with each of the texts before beginning their answers.

- Both sections of this paper (COMPREHENDING and COMPOSING) must be attempted.
- Each section carries 100 marks.

### SECTION I – COMPREHENDING

- Two Questions, A and B, follow each text.
- Candidates must answer a Question A on one text and a Question B on a different text. Candidates must answer only one Question A and only one Question B.
- **N.B.** Candidates may NOT answer a Question A and a Question B on the same text.

### SECTION II – COMPOSING

- Candidates must write on **one** of the compositions 1 – 7.

## Section 1 Comprehending (100 marks)
- **Three reading choices are given**, one of which is a set of pictures. There will be a common theme to all three texts, although this makes no difference in answering questions.
- **Read one text and answer the Question A that follows it.** Question A carries 50 marks and is usually broken into three short questions (15 marks + 15 marks + 20 marks).
- **Read a different text and answer the Question B that follows it.** Question B also carries 50 marks, but it is usually a longer question inspired by the text. It can be a speech, diary, report, newspaper article, advertisement, etc.

Question A (50 marks) + Question B (50 marks) = Total for Comprehending (100 marks)

## Section 2 Composing (100 marks)
- The Composing section is sometimes called '**the essay question**'.
- There are **seven options of compositions** and they are inspired by the three reading choices in Section 1.
- Compositions carry **100 marks**.
- Three or four options will be **narratives**, e.g. 'write a story'.
- Other options are **similar to Question B in Section 1** (e.g. write a speech, report or article) but are longer.
- One option will be **inspired by the pictures** in the Section 1: Comprehension.

Total for Composing (100 marks)

# Paper 2

Paper 2 has three sections:

## Section 1 Single text option (60 marks)
- Your **teacher chooses a text** (novel or play) to be studied in detail.
- You must answer **three short questions** on specific moments or issues in the story (10 marks + 10 marks + 10 marks = 30 marks).
- You must answer **one longer question** that requires analysis of bigger issues in the story. You will be given three longer questions to choose from and each will carry equal marks. Choose one to answer (30 marks).
- This is the text that you need to be most familiar with for the exam.

Three short questions (30 marks) + one longer question (30 marks) = Total for Single Text Option (60 marks)

# EXAM OUTLINE AND MENTAL PREPARATION

## Section 2 Comparative study (70 marks)
- Your **teacher chooses two or three texts** (novels, plays or films).
- You **compare the texts** under specific headings or 'modes'.
- **Modes include:** theme (2014/2015); relationships (2014/2015); social setting (2014) hero-heroine-villain (2015).
- **Three** such modes are **prescribed** for the exam each year.
- **Two of the three modes will appear on the paper.**
- **Choose one** of the two modes in the exam, **either A or B**.
- Each mode is usually broken into two parts: **Q1 or Q2. Choose one.**
- It is important to read all of these questions carefully and **make a good choice before you write anything**.
- You will have two questions under the same mode on the texts you have studied. The marks are usually divided into **30 marks + 40 marks** (70 marks).

**Total for Comparative Study (70 marks)**

## Section 3 Poetry (70 marks)

### A Unseen poem (20 marks)
- Usually a short and interesting poem that you read closely.
- Questions follow the poem. Sometimes there are two short questions of 10 marks each. Sometimes there is one longer question of 20 marks.

### B Prescribed poetry (50 marks)
- There are 36 poems prescribed on the course.
- The poems are divided into two sections: 20 poems come from a combined higher/ordinary level list and 16 poems come from a list of poems for ordinary level only.
- Teachers and students must be clear about which list of poems they will study closely. Revise one list or the other. There is no need to study 36 poems.
- Four poems will appear on the exam paper: two from one list and two from the other. Choose one poem on which to answer questions.
- Questions follow each poem. Typically they involve three short questions of 10 marks each, followed by one longer question of 20 marks.
- The question carrying 20 marks often asks you to be creative in your response, as opposed to simply explaining what the poem means.

**A: Unseen Poem (20 marks) + B: Prescribed Poetry (50 marks) = Total for Poetry Section (70 marks).**

**Grand Total = 400 Marks**

## The day of the exam

Traditionally, the Leaving Certificate exam schedule has begun on the first Wednesday after the June bank holiday. You will be given English Paper 1 just before 9.30am that day. Thousands of students from all walks of life are given the opportunity to have their knowledge, understanding, skills and attitudes assessed and rewarded.

### Nerves

Most students will be nervous, but that is not a bad thing! **Nervousness can be a powerfully positive force in pressure situations.** Believe it or not, it is good to be nervous. By using this book, you will learn how to turn nerves into powerful and effective writing.

Being **nervous** is physiological, which means it is something to do with your body's reaction to a pressure situation. Being **afraid** is different. It is a psychological state, which means that it is in your head. While both are interlinked, the physical signs of nervousness are an indication that you are physically prepared for the challenge. **Your body and your brain are ready to perform!**

Keep a positive attitude when revising. Try to enjoy the challenge of reading and writing.

You might experience: sweaty palms as you hold your pen; increased heart rate as you await the paper; and a funny feeling in your stomach. All of these signs are **normal and healthy**. Remember that anybody who ever achieved anything of great merit felt exactly the same way. Most students in the exam hall will feel this way, too. So don't get upset by being nervous. It is the way most people will feel.

## The three Cs

### Clarity

Clarity means being **clear**. It is absolutely essential that you are clear about what the English exam entails and also what each individual question asks of you. Each chapter in this book will begin with a set of **aims**. Examine the aims closely, so that you **know what you are trying to achieve**. Throughout the book, typical questions for each section will be outlined. Sample answers will be provided, along with close detail on how such answers are graded. A timing guide will also be given and key points will be emphasised. All of these elements will ensure that you have clarity.

To write well, you need: **CLARITY, COHERENCE** and **CONFIDENCE**. These elements are reflected in the marking scheme.

## Coherence

Coherence means **making sense**. Having worked out what each exam question means, the aim is to write coherent answers. Many teachers and examiners will tell you that students frequently fail to **answer the question asked**. Others fail to answer the right number of questions or simply do not **make sensible choices in the exam** itself. If you have worries about spelling and grammar, try to focus on answering the right questions and making sense. You will be rewarded.

## Confidence

Every student desires confidence. It is actually nothing more than **your feelings about yourself**. If you think you are no good at something, then you are very likely to be no good. However, the reverse is not necessarily true: thoughts of greatness and brilliance are not enough by themselves. **In order to increase your confidence, you must keep reading and practising your writing.** Then what you write, and how you write it, will be greatly improved. Examiners look for answers that show a broad command of English as well as a student's individual way of responding. If you work hard and feel confident, your efforts will pay off.

Having a **positive attitude** is the starting point for getting good grades in your exams.

Each of the chapters devoted to an aspect of the exam will follow these three Cs as an outline for revision.

# 2 The Marking Scheme

- To understand exactly how the exam is marked, through detailed analysis of two comprehension answers.
- To show the link between **content** (what you write) and **style** (how you write).

## How the exam is marked

Examiners do not mark your work according to their opinion or guesswork. Every answer is marked according to specific headings outlined below.

Always aim to write as much as you can in the time allowed, once it is relevant to the question.

### Note
Examiners' Assessments appear throughout the book. You will notice that these contain a breakdown of marks awarded. Marking is done by reference to the **PCLM** criteria for assessment:

- Clarity of purpose (P):            30% of the total.
- Coherence of delivery (C):         30% of the total.
- Efficiency of language use (L):    30% of the total.
- Accuracy of mechanics (M):         10% of the total.

## Clarity of purpose (30%)

This is explained as 'engagement with the set task', which is a fancy way of asking whether or not you have **answered the question that was asked**. It also means that you must have a **personal, original answer**. Your answer should not be learned off word for word from notes. You will be rewarded for honesty and for sticking to what the question asks of you. For example, when you are asked if you **like or dislike the Unseen Poem**, the first sentence of your answer should immediately state **whether you do or don't**. This should be followed by your reasons and backed up with quotations and support.

## Coherence of delivery (30%)

This aspect concerns structure. Have you **constructed your answer in a logical fashion** with statement, quotation and comment? Do you **make sense** from beginning to end? You are expected to deal with one point per paragraph and to have your ideas ordered in a logical sequence. For example, essays should have a clear beginning, middle and end.

THE MARKING SCHEME

## Efficiency of language use (30%)

This refers to your vocabulary, your fluency with words and your phrasing of ideas. In simple terms, it is **how** you write, as opposed to **what** you write. You can never have enough practice in this area. Language skills often determine your final grade.

## Accuracy of mechanics (10%)

This refers to spelling and grammar, as well as the correct placement of words in sentences. While you won't be penalised for every error, **poor mechanics can have a negative effect on your overall grade**.

| | SIMPLE GUIDE | |
|---|---|---|
| 1. | Answer the question asked | (30%) |
| 2. | Make sense in your answer | (30%) |
| 3. | Use good vocabulary and expressions | (30%) |
| 4. | Spell correctly | (10%) |

In each answer, candidates are asked to:

- Display a clear and purposeful engagement with the set task. (P)
- Sustain the response in an appropriate manner over the entire answer. (C)
- Manage and control language appropriate to the task. (L)
- Display levels of accuracy in spelling and grammar appropriate to the required/chosen register. (M)

**key point**

The **content** of your answer (**what** you write) covers 60% of the total marks in every question. The **style** (**how** you write) counts for 40%.

Observe how each Sample Answer is marked according to PCLM throughout the book and try to make your own answers more exam-focused!

The following comprehension is from the 2009 exam. The 15-mark question from Part A relates to the extract. You can read a student's sample answer and the examiner's assessment of it.

### YouTube – CONNECTING OUR WORLD

Irish Independent journalist, Gemma O'Doherty, interviewed Chad Hurley. He, along with his partners, Steve Chen and Jawed Karim, came up with an idea which has connected millions of people on the website, YouTube. The following edited extract is based on that interview.

### Q1. How did YouTube come about?

YouTube started with such a simple idea. We had videos we wanted to share with our families and friends but found there wasn't really a way of doing that on the internet. We thought it would be interesting to see if we could figure out a way that would make it simple to share home-made video material. My friend Steve Chen and I put our heads together and started coming up with new ways of putting video onto the net. We wanted to give our website mass appeal, to make our website easy to use, without the need for any special software.

Most importantly we did not charge people for the service. Within months the site was flooded with videos and there was no shortage of viewers willing to watch them. They were able to send each other links to the website. We were in the right place at the right time. People had started getting their own devices, like mobile phones and digital cameras, which enabled them to make videos to share with one another. We knew we were on to something special.

### Q2. Why is YouTube so popular?

The website has become the first stop for young people who want to watch a video on the internet. Thanks to YouTube, the dream of creating television on demand suddenly became a reality. Every single minute, ten hours of new material ranging from shaky home videos to concert clips, is put onto the website. It is a place where ordinary people can be turned into celebrities with an audience of 100 million viewers.

### Q3. What makes YouTube so successful?

This is a multi-tasking generation. Young people are capable of dealing with multiple things at once. They're not just sitting behind their computer; at the same time they may be watching TV or talking on their mobile phone or reading a magazine. The internet revolution is all about connecting people. If you look at the success of social networking, like Facebook or text messaging or email, it's all about communication. That has been the key to YouTube's success. It's a great way to connect with other people. What we're seeing with this generation is the sharing of ideas, thoughts and experiences.

### Q4. How do you protect your website from misuse?

We are fully aware that the website has the potential to be dangerous. We have made it clear what's acceptable to put on YouTube and what's not. Content that is violent or hateful or generally unsuitable we can remove in a matter of minutes.

### Q5. What does the future hold for YouTube?

People are always going to want quality information and entertainment, be it from newspapers, television or magazines and certainly that demand is not going to disappear. YouTube is adding to the choice. We are continuing to work on our website which is still so young. The speed of connection to the website will continue to improve. It will be increasingly possible to connect from wherever you are at any time. It's a chance for different cultures to talk to each other. Every day YouTube gets bigger and as a result I'm working harder!

## THE MARKING SCHEME

### Question A
Having read the entire interview, what do you think are the advantages and disadvantages of YouTube? Support your answer with reference to the text.

(15 marks)

Now read the student's answer and the examiner's assessment of it. Before reading the examiner's assessment, try to work out the mark that you think the student deserves. See if you are close to the actual mark.

**SAMPLE ANSWER: A**

[Poor opening statement] **One of the advantages of youtube are the connections other people can make among fellow viewers of youtube** as he says 'it is a place where [Poor spelling] **ordunarey** people can be turned into celebrites with an audience of 100 million **viewers'** also it is a great way to share videos with family members and friends, The disadvantages would be with unstuable videos that Chad Huyrly says 'content that is violent or hateful or generally unsuitable we can remove in a matter of minutes' but with some people on u-tube over 100,000 people could watch that video **in that minute stated**. [Poor grammar] [Weak expression]

(100 words approx.)

For 15-mark questions, the first two headings (clarity of purpose and coherence of delivery) are combined. The last two headings (language and mechanics) are also combined. **This happens for all questions with fewer than 30 marks.**

Marks are then divided **60/40**. This gives **9 marks** for **what** is written and **6 marks** for **how** it is written (15 marks in total).

Is it a good answer?

**EXAMINER'S ASSESSMENT**

- The student answers the question asked and provides some quotation. So **an attempt is made and it is broadly correct**.
- The answer is approximately 100 words long, with no distinct paragraphing. It is **minimum content** for a 15-mark question.
- The content of the answer is **basic** and of **average to poor quality**.
- **Language and mechanics are quite poor here.** Quotes are inaccurate; names are spelled incorrectly; the vocabulary is basic; and the structure is poor, with only one full stop used in the whole answer.
- Marks: 4 (P and C) + 2 (L and M) = 6/15 (D3 grade).

As you can see, this is not a particularly good answer. However, it manages to meet the minimum pass mark

**key point**

**Effort** is rewarded at ordinary level. Answer the question asked as best you can in the time allowed.

of 40%. A student continuing to write like this in the exam would run the serious risk of failing.

Now look at Question B. Of course, in the real exam you can't choose Question A and Question B on the same text extract! A different student's response is given for Question B.

In this case, the four aspects of marking (purpose, coherence, language and mechanics) are divided separately to give a breakdown of 15 + 15 + 15 + 5 = 50 marks. **This is the case for all questions with 30 marks or more.**

## Question B

You have won a competition entitled 'Be a Celebrity for a Day'. Write out two diary entries or two blog entries about your experience.

(50 marks)

### SAMPLE ANSWER: B

**Tuesday 14th – Morning** ◀ *Proper diary heading*

Woke up as usual, but today is anything but the usual. Needed to shake myself extra hard to **get myself ready** ◀ *Suitably casual tone* for the big adventure ahead. Ignored my tangled hair for once. I had to get the rest of my head around the idea first. Dad loves clichés but when he said 'it's not every day you meet Brad Pitt' he was right for once. Ever since that 'Be A Celebrity For A Day' contest caught my eye six weeks ago, I knew I had the edge. I reckon I could have a career in the media some day. I have that star quality that those talent spotters speak of. It will start today with this new coffee commercial, alongside the **super-suave** Brad. ◀ *Alliteration*
Oh my God, in three hours I will be standing next to handsomeness himself, probably blabbering and **stumbling over myself** ◀ *Good expression* like some thirteen-year-old on her first date. I've never worked in an advertising agency before. This is an amazing way to begin a new career. I just hope Brad understands this too. Maybe he will talk to me? I'm sure he has met countless thousands of girls before, all **ogling** ◀ *Excellent verb* him and doing the **usual flirting thing**. But I'm going to be different. I'm a total amateur, but I'm gonna try to be a true ◀ *Suitably casual language* professional. Speaking of which, it's now nearly two hours to the launch. Need to get this hair straightened fairly lively.

# THE MARKING SCHEME

Evening

I'm back. Or should that be 'stand back' cos **I'm fit to kill somebody right now!** Thank God for diaries. I know Mother says they are very useful for dealing with issues but right now I would gladly **wallop** Brad Pitt to death with this one. Issues? What a total sleaze! I told him loads of times my name was Sandra but he kept calling me Sindy and patting me on the head **like I'm some plaything or pet kitten**. He ignored me when I asked how to stand, speak, walk, move and smile. And when he dropped the coffee pot, he said it was 'the dumb blonde's fault', i.e. ME, who supposedly distracted him when I bent down! I was following the director and concentrating on my lines while he looked like he wanted the quickest flight back to California or Cambodia, or **whatever other hole he lives in these days**. Well I hope he falls down some hole because he has ruined all the excitement I had in me. So much for a media career. Right now I couldn't care less.

(420 words approx.)

- Good change of tone
- Expressive verb
- Simile
- Colourful expression

## EXAMINER'S ASSESSMENT

- This is an excellent effort. At over 400 words, it is certainly long enough and it covers two diary entries as required.
- The register (language, tone, purpose) is appropriate to a diary and it is original in that it does not suggest a happy outcome to a supposedly happy event. This deserves good marks.
- It is structured well. Two different moments in the day capture a teenage girl's reactions to the day's events.
- Vocabulary is of an excellent standard. The use of 'cos' and 'gonna' is appropriate to the diary format. Simile and alliteration are used effectively.
- Very few spelling/grammar errors.
- Marks: 15 (P) + 13 (C) + 13 (L) + 5 (M) = 46/50 (A1 Grade).

**exam focus**

Visit www.examinations.ie for further details on how the exam is marked.

**exam focus**

Questions with greater marks challenge you more. Practise the shorter questions first and apply the same method to longer ones later.

# 3 Language Genres in the Exam

**aims** — To learn about the different genres of language that appear in the exam.

Think about one of the text extracts that appeared in previous chapters of this book. Did you find it: boring, uninteresting, non-stimulating, useful, intriguing, thought-provoking, logical, factual or descriptive? Perhaps it was none of these. But did you notice that there were nine different adjectives suggested to describe a possible reaction to the piece?

Your own reaction could be completely different from all of these suggestions. This illustrates the variety and beauty that is found in the English language. We employ an enormous range of words in our speaking and writing; more than any other language on earth. We also classify language types or **genres**. In studying Leaving Certificate Ordinary Level English, you need to be familiar with five genres:

1. **Informative language:** the language of information.
2. **Narrative language:** the language of story.
3. **Persuasive language:** the language of persuasion.
4. **Argumentative language:** the language of logic.
5. **Aesthetic language:** the language of beauty and style.

- **Informative language** is all around you. It is **direct, factual, objective** and should be **easy to understand**. You will employ lots of informative language in your exam answers.
- **Narrative language** is found in **stories, diaries** and **personal essays**. Not all students who like to tell stories are necessarily good at writing them. (Chapter 5 will help you to make this decision for yourself.)
- **Persuasive language** attempts to put forward a point of view or opinion in a way that might **influence** other people. It is often **emotive**. This means that it touches people's **feelings** more than their logic or sense. It is used in political speeches and is essential in good advertising and various other strands of the media. It is likely that you will use persuasive language in many of your answers.
- **Argumentative language** is the language of logic and argument. It is less concerned with emotive language than with **logical, rational** thought and speech. A **debate** is by definition an argument. While argument tries to remain cold and **factual**,

persuasion contains more emotion and suggestion. You may find questions in Paper 2 that ask you to argue for or against a viewpoint. The wording of these questions often contains the phrase: 'Do you agree with …?'

- **Aesthetic language** is found in works of **literature**, such as poetry, drama and cinema. It is considered **beautiful** or **stylish** language and can be called 'aesthetically pleasing'. This quality gives writing its colour, humour, power and vitality.

These five language genres are all around you every day. The more you read and the more you look, the more you will recognise them.

# Recognising the genres

What follows are **five short passages**, all of which refer to the same concept: a cake. In each case, identify which of the genres is being used.

1. Cakes are an essential feature of most modern wedding celebrations. I would argue that to replace such a standard cake with a jelly and ice-cream monstrosity is illogical and foolish. I also fear that it will cause an unwanted mess due to its likely melting before the main course is finished.

2. Take the cake mixture, already well settled, and place in a grease proof baking dish. Smooth around the edges and ensure that none of the mixture contains lumps. Cover with a baking sheet and place in a preheated oven at 180 degrees centigrade. Cook for two hours, or until the top is golden and crispy. Allow to settle before removing from the dish.

3. The scoop of the spoon, the bend of the bowl. The sweep of mother's hand as she gathers the precious remaining grains of flavour into her cloudy, floury fingers. With a final few stirs and whips, the molten mixture is ready for its final journey to the cavernous oven. Then the real moment of tension: the split second before mother tosses the utensils to the waiting sink. It is all the time he needs. With an innocent, pleading grin, he gently swipes the sugar-and-dough coated delicacy. Wooden spoons never tasted so good.

4. The day Henry decided to bake his own wedding cake was the day it started to go wrong. While it might seem inappropriate now to blame divorce on such trivial matters, wars have been fought over less. Anyway, Henry was a stubborn type, insisting on an ice-cream monstrosity despite advice from those who knew better.

5. As one who speaks for the marginalised of this society, I implore you all to donate any unwanted cakes for the upcoming charity cake sale. Your company produces more than five hundred cakes a week, some of which end up being thrown to the bins because of a lack of demand from your regular customers. Can you really continue with this thoughtless policy, as others beg for scraps of food to survive? You have the power to bring about change.

**Did you notice the specific features of each genre?**

1. **Argumentative** language appeals to logic and sense, e.g. a jelly and ice-cream cake is likely to melt.
2. **Informative** language is mostly factual. In this case, we read that the instructions for successfully baking a cake are given.
3. **Aesthetic** language rises above the ordinary and the purely informative. This beautiful and colourful description of a childhood memory stimulates our imagination.
4. **Narrative** language tells a story, as in the story of poor Henry whose stubbornness gets him into trouble.
5. **Persuasive** language tugs at your feelings, e.g. pleading with the reader to consider the needy in society.

> **exam focus**
> If you are familiar with different language genres, you will find it easier to answer questions.

Your teacher has probably helped you become familiar with examples of each genre. In many cases, a piece of writing will contain **combinations** of the above. For practice, reread chapter one and find examples of each genre.

# Paper 1

# 4 Comprehension

- To examine the **types of questions** that occur in the Comprehension section.
- To understand the importance of **choosing the questions wisely** before answering any of them'

While the Comprehension section appears straightforward, it does amount to **25 per cent of your final total**, so treat it with care and caution.

Comprehension means to understand something. The Comprehension section is a fairly gentle start to your Leaving Certificate, since the questions aim to test your ability to respond logically and creatively to questions on a given text.

Three or four different **extracts** will appear on the exam paper. Two of these will consist of a written piece, usually from a magazine, book, newspaper or other source. The other text will be a selection of visuals (pictures) for you to examine.

**key point**
If you choose the *same* text for Question A and Question B, you are guaranteed to lose **at least 50 marks**, which is 12.5 per cent of the total. This can mean a serious drop in your final grade. Do not make this mistake!

There are two types of questions to answer:

- **Question A**: broken into three parts and amounting to 50 marks in total.
- **Question B**: a single question requiring a longer answer and also amounting to 50 marks in total.

You must choose one Question A for one text and one Question B for a different text.

## How to approach the comprehension section

Take time to **read all of the comprehensions. Choose your Question B first.** This is a more demanding exercise, so you should pick the one you feel best suits you. Then select your **Question A**. The standard is similar across all questions. **Once your choice is made,** answer Question A and then Question B. The most important rule for Comprehension questions is: **answer the question asked.**

## Language genres in the comprehension section

**Choose your questions carefully!** Choose Question B, then choose Question A. Once you've made your choice, complete Question A first, then Question B.

### Informative language

All of the texts contain information. This is factual, impersonal language. It is not emotive and it speaks directly, e.g. *Hamlet was the Prince of Denmark.* **It is most likely that A Questions will ask you to locate specific pieces of information in the given text.**

### Narrative language

This language tells a story. Clearly you need information to tell a story, so there will be some crossover with informative language here. But narration happens in a time and place (setting) and uses words to create situations, images, feelings and reactions. For example: *I will always remember the day that I broke my leg.* **Narration is likely to be found in B Questions.**

### Persuasive language

Persuasion involves one-sided opinion, often with emotion attached. You might remember your Junior Certificate Media Studies section. It highlighted the role of persuasive language in advertising, along with buzz words and slogans, e.g. *8 out of 10 cats prefer it; Unbeatable value at our new store; The time for change has come, etc.* **B questions that involve a talk with an audience, advertisement scripts or political speeches must all involve persuasive language.**

### Argumentative language

An argument presents facts in a clear, logical and convincing way. For example: *Uniforms should be compulsory in schools for the following three reasons...* Each of your A answers should read like a short argument, where you tackle the question by using evidence selected from the text. **Most comprehension exercises involve arguing your point in a logical and clear way.** B questions, such as a debate or journalistic article, are likely to involve argument.

### Aesthetic language

All good writing is aesthetically pleasing, even if you don't immediately recognise this quality. But what is aesthetic language? A simple way of understanding this is to ask: **does it sound good to read?** This happens when we write answers as if we were artists enjoying our work, rather than students struggling to succeed.

'Students struggling to succeed' is a simple example of alliteration, an aesthetic feature. 'The exam is a marathon' is a metaphor. 'The exam hall is like a pressure cooker' is a simile. All of these features of language show how we can elevate and improve our expression through the use of aesthetics. You can write like this too!

# Comprehension: A Questions

These short questions ask the following:

- **What** is the writer saying?
- **How** does the writer say it?
- What is your **response** to it?

They are marked out of either 15 or 20 marks. You must write a little more and think a little more carefully about 20-mark questions. It is a good idea to read the questions first, **underlining key words** to help you work out the purpose. This allows your mind extra time to **subconsciously** figure out answers as you read.

The following comprehension and questions are from the 2006 exam. You can read a student's sample answers and the examiner's assessments. Try reading the questions before you read the extract – see if it helps to focus your mind.

**INVASION!**

**This story is adapted from John Wyndham's *The Kraken Wakes*. It is a story of the invasion from outer space by an alien life form trying to destroy the human race. In this extract, Mike, the narrator, and Phyl, his girlfriend, are investigating the problem on the island of Escondida in the Gulf of Mexico. They are relaxing and listening to a guitarist when …**

**1**

Suddenly the evening changed as the distant player dropped his guitar with a clang. Down by the waterfront a voice called out. I could not make it out but it was alarming. Then we heard the sound of breaking crockery. A woman screamed. We turned to look at the houses that screened the little harbour. 'Listen!' said Phyl. 'Mike, do you think—?' She broke off at the sound of a machine gun firing. 'It must be! Mike, they must be coming!'

**2**

There was an increasing racket in the distance. In the Square itself windows were opening, people calling questions from one to another. Half a dozen soldiers arrived carrying a rocket launcher and laid themselves down on the cobbles, their weapon aimed at the opening to the Square. Except for a few sounds of sobbing, a tense expectant silence held the whole scene. And then in the background one became aware of a grinding, scraping noise; not loud but deep and threatening.

**3**

Then we had our first sight of an alien. It was like a huge dark beetle, a curve of dull, grey metal sliding into the Square, demolishing a shop-front as it came. More rockets were fired but they seemed to thud into the metal without any effect. Slowly, heavily, this strange shape was joined by two others in the Square. They seemed to move into position like troops about to attack. 'Look!' said Phyl. 'This one's bulging.' She was pointing to the nearest one. The previously smooth surface at the top of the sea-tank began to bulge and out came a large white ball. 'They're all doing it now – look, and there's two more,' screamed Phyl.

**4**

Slowly the first ball began to float in our direction and then suddenly something happened to it. It did not exactly explode. Nor was there any sound. Rather it seemed to turn inside out with a vast number of long white arms like an octopus waving in the air. Our instinctive reaction was to jump back from the window away from it. We did. Four or five of the arms, like long white whiplashes, flicked in through the window and dropped to the floor. Almost as they touched it they began to withdraw except for one that had grasped Phyl's foot. It was already contracting, pulling her towards the window. She pulled back. 'Mike!' she cried. 'O Mike!' The thing was tugging hard and she had already been dragged a couple of yards towards the window. She rolled to one side and tore at the arm. For a second it let go of her as if to get a better grip. I grabbed a kitchen knife, rushed towards her and brought it down with full force cutting it in two. It and its companions withdrew.

**5**

But outside in the Square there was complete chaos. With nowhere to escape to, people were being caught by the arms. I saw a man rush forward to try to pull a screaming woman away, but when he touched the arm of this thing, another instantly flashed out and grabbed him. Both were pulled along the street. I will never forget their dying screams.

**6**

It was morning before the attack ended. Strangely there were no bodies to recover although hundreds had been killed. On the news we heard of many attacks on coastal towns throughout the world. It would be many months before the world would sleep easy again; many months before these monsters were defeated.

## Question A

(i) What happened in part 1 of this story that ended the quietness of the evening? Give a reason.

(15 marks)

(ii) How does the writer show the atmosphere of tension and fear in parts 2 and 3 of the extract?

(15 marks)

(iii) Which of the six sections of this story would make the best material for a scene in a film called Invasion!? Give reasons for your choice.

(20 marks)

It's useful to underline or highlight the **key words** in each question. This would produce the following results:

(i) What happened ... part 1 ... ended the quietness ... reason.

(ii) How ... tension and fear ... parts 2 and 3.

(iii) Which ... sections ... best material ... scene in a ... film ... reasons.

These questions neatly follow the typical format of comprehension A Questions. You are often asked: **what** happened; **how** is it written; and what is your **response** to what you have read.

Let's examine **question (i)** in more detail. It asks what happened to end the quietness. We can list several reasons that the quietness ended:

- A voice called out.
- Crockery was broken.
- A woman screamed.
- Machine gun fire rang out.

These four items of information can be put together in a coherent answer. Read the sample answer below.

### SAMPLE ANSWER: A (i)

**In part 1, four different and distinct noises break the evening quietness. First, a 'voice calls out' from the waterfront. It is followed by the sound of 'broken crockery' and then a 'woman screaming'. Then, as Phyl and Mike wonder what is happening, they hear the sound of a 'machine gun firing'. All together, these sounds disturb what was up to that point a relaxing and quiet evening for the characters.**

(70 words approx.)

### EXAMINER'S ASSESSMENT

- This is a top-grade effort: well-phrased and providing the relevant information in a clear and logical fashion.
- Marks: 9 (P and C) + 6 (L and M) = 15/15 (A1 grade).

Look closely at **question (ii)**. It asks how the author shows an atmosphere of tension and fear in parts 2 and 3. The author does this in many ways:

- Descriptive language evokes vivid (strong and clear) imagery and suggests something frightening.
- Short, snappy sentences hint at what is happening. Authors often use this technique to create tension.
- The author appeals to our senses. Tension and fear relate to how you feel, what you hear and what you see. The author's awareness of this makes for greater effect.

We can use all of the information above to create a coherent answer. Read the sample answer below. Note that both tension and fear are covered in the answer, as they are closely related.

### SAMPLE ANSWER: A (ii)

**In part 2, the writer creates fear by using words that suggest something bad is about to happen. There is an 'increasing racket' as soldiers arrive with a 'rocket launcher'. In the background, we are made aware of a 'grinding, scraping noise; not loud but deep and threatening'. The fear increases when the alien arrives in part 3. He is huge, dark, dull and grey and the rockets do not stop his advances. Two more aliens then join him and the characters Phyl and Mike seemed destined to die. Tension is evident in part 2 when the 'tense expectant silence' is felt just before the attack begins. In part 3, the bulging balls hint at the creation of even more alien invaders. 'Look!' said Phyl. 'This one's bulging.' This short sentence communicates the moment of tension before the exciting appearance of more alien life to the devastated scene.**

(150 words approx.)

### EXAMINER'S ASSESSMENT
- Top marks here for the excellent use of quotation. Each quote is indicated by proper quotation marks and is written exactly as it appears in the text.
- Marks: 9 (P and C) + 6 (L and M) = 15/15 (A1 grade).

**Question (iii)** asks which section would be suitable material for a film. In truth, any of the sections could be used in a film. This question is really a test of your expression and opinion on the piece. Let's examine section 4 for this answer, since it contains many features of an exciting action movie scene. For example:

- Conflict.
- Dialogue.
- Dramatic action.
- A heroic rescue.

### SAMPLE ANSWER: A (iii)

**Any of the sections could fit with an action film script. I would choose number 4, since it contains the moment of most drama and excitement. The essential conflict of the film – the alien versus mankind scenario – reaches its highpoint here. The alien tries to attack Phyl and almost drags her away. Mike comes to her rescue with a knife. This could be played out as an action sequence with dramatic music in the background. Also, the alien appears from inside some kind of ball. It has five arms and is very ugly. This requires lots of special effects to be used and such effects are a central part of science fiction films nowadays. There is also room for some dramatic dialogue as Phyl is taken away, so this scene would allow us to see Mike as the hero at this moment. Finally, people like to be excited**

and entertained by films. For this, we need tension to occur. There is much tension at this moment, which will make us want to see how it finishes. All of these features make this section the most suitable for a film version.

(190 words approx.)

### EXAMINER'S ASSESSMENT

- This is the longest of the three answers, since it carries 20 marks. Four distinct reasons are put forward for the candidate's opinion. Each reason is backed up with reference from the text (even if there is no direct quotation).
- Marks: 12 (P and C) + 8 (L and M) = 20/20 (A1 grade).

Overall grade for Question A is 50/50 (A1 grade).

The student who **digs deep into a small section** of the text can do just as well as the student who provides wide analysis of the entire article. **Look at the small details as well as the major points**.

## Comprehension: B Questions

B Questions could be considered 'short essay' questions. These questions test your personal writing skills within a closely defined task. Therefore you must always bear in mind **what the task is**.

Each B Question will have:

- A specific **purpose**: what you must write.
- A stated **audience**: to whom the piece is addressed.
- A particular **register**: the piece must sound right.

Remember this as a golfer would: you are trying to score a **par** on each question. Always know your purpose, audience and register for each question on Paper 1.

PURPOSE, AUDIENCE AND REGISTER

The **purpose** and the **audience** will be indicated in the question itself. Close reading of the questions will reveal them to you.

However, **register** is more difficult to define. The scenarios below will help you to understand and find the right register:

- Imagine speaking to a small child and explaining something complicated. You will use certain words and phrases and take a gentle tone in order to be understood. You would not speak the same way to an adult about the same issue. You expect that the adult will understand differently, so you change your language and tone to suit the audience.

- Explaining the economic situation to a group of students in university will require lots of factual analysis and statistical data. A politician explaining the economic situation to voters will need a much more careful (and perhaps emotive) approach in order to be understood.

Register is a blend of suitable **vocabulary, tone** and **treatment of the task**.

## Types of B Questions

By looking at past papers, you will notice that some B Questions require similar answers. They can be grouped into types in order to help with revision and practice.

### 1. Writing for media

Examples include:

- Review
- Newspaper article
- Report
- Commentary on an event
- Advertisement script.

This type of question involves writing for the media. Questions can take many forms, but there are overall similarities within the type.

If you like to read newspapers, blog or follow current affairs, a media-type question may suit you. Perhaps there is a journalist or sports commentator inside you waiting to get out! If you like **expressing opinions to a broad audience**, consider this option on the exam paper.

In questions that involve writing for media, there is bound to be lots of opinion. Sometimes **bias** can occur when a writer takes a very one-sided view of a situation. Since this is a creative exercise, a one-sided view could make for very good reading, e.g. a sports commentator with a very strong preference for one team over another can write very entertaining pieces.

# COMPREHENSION

This Question B is taken from the 2006 paper.

## Question B
Write a review for your school magazine of any film that you have enjoyed. Your review should encourage other students to go see it.

(50 marks)

This question can be broken down as follows:

**Task:** Review for a school magazine.

**Purpose:** To write a review that encourages people to see the film.

**Audience:** Student population.

**Register:** This should include:

- **Informative language**: Name of film, actors, director, setting, context and some plot details.
- **Persuasion**: Positive attitude to the film, reasons to see it and positive comparisons with other films.
- **Purpose**: The purpose of the piece is to convince your audience of the film's merits.
- **Tone**: It may be useful to use a **light-hearted, conversational tone**, since you want to connect with your young audience and not sound too self-important or overly critical.

Short reviews of recent movies are often found on the back of DVD covers. Theatre and concert reviews can be found on billboard advertisements and in publicity for the shows. You can learn a lot about suitable register from these items.

## SAMPLE ANSWER: B

### *Avatar 3D* (2009)
### Directed by James Cameron

Director James Cameron does not make films too often. But when he does, they tend to leave a lasting mark on cinema critics and audiences alike. My recent trip to the cinema was to experience his **futuristic** three-hour epic *Avatar*, showing in its 3D format for added enjoyment.

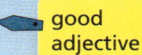
good adjective

Was it worth the long sit and the **obligatory** 3D glasses? That answer is easy. It is simply the best film I've seen – or should I say 'experienced' – this year.

[good adjective]

But what it is about this film that has audiences enthralled? Where do we start? Perhaps we could mention the plot, which was simple enough, despite **the long running time of 166 minutes**. In the future, injured marine Jake Sully decides to take a place on a mission to the distant world of Pandora. He assumes an 'avatar' existence – one where he fits in perfectly with the local inhabitants, the Na'vi. While there, he learns of greedy villain Parker Selfridge's intentions of driving off the semi-human Na'vi creatures, in order to mine for the precious material scattered throughout their rich woodland. While Jake begins to bond with the native tribe, he quickly falls in love with the beautiful alien Neytiri. **The soldier then must take a stand and fight back in an epic battle for the fate of Pandora**.

[important information]

[sentence captures the excitement]

The cast is led by Sam Worthington in the role of hero. This was a fairly unknown list of actors, except for Sigourney Weaver, whose role here is similar to **her part of unlikely heroine in the *Alien* films**. Perhaps the director was more concerned with the stunning visual effects than having a big box-office star stealing the limelight. Whatever the case, Worthington and co-stars (Zoe Saldana as Neytiri and Giovanni Ribisi as Selfridge) keep us rooted to our seats as we wait to see the fate of Pandora.

[indicates knowledge of cinema]

The sets, graphic depiction, sound-editing and art direction are simply outstanding. **Love, action, storyline, visual effects, sound effects, hair, make-up, aliens, humanoids, weapons** – the list of features goes on. This is a film that will appeal to all types of moviegoers. Just make sure to include the 3D glasses for that something extra.

[lists film's strong points]

**A resounding five-star rating**.

[excellent concluding expression]

(370 words approx.)

### EXAMINER'S ASSESSMENT

- This answer has all the elements necessary for a review. It comments on both the content and style of the film.
- The purpose has been adhered to: the review encourages the readers to see the film.
- The first two paragraphs are mostly informative. A more persuasive tone is used later in the piece.
- The standard of vocabulary and knowledge of cinema create a very high standard.
- Marks: 15 (P) + 15 (C) + 15 (L) + 5 (M) = 50/50 (A1 grade).

## 2. Letters and diary entries

These answers must be written with the assumption that very few people, if any, will get to read them. They are often much more **personal** and **intimate** than other forms. Sometimes they can be **formal**, as in a formal or business letter.

If you feel comfortable **expressing your feelings** in a diary, or if you write letters when the opportunity arises, you should consider this type of question. Some people find it **easier to write things down** rather than say them directly to another person. If you are like this, letters and diary entries might be suitable forms for you.

Revise the section on **diary entries** in Chapter 2. Study the example, sample answer and marking scheme there. Below you will find more information on **letters**.

This Question B appeared on the 2008 paper, accompanying the first comprehension piece.

### Question B
Imagine that you live beside the 'neighbours from hell'. Write the letter that you would send to the police complaining about this problem.

(50 marks)

This question can be broken down as follows:

**Task:** Formal letter in the proper format and register.

**Purpose:** To complain about your neighbours from hell.

**Audience:** Local Gardaí – nobody else will see it.

**Register:** Formal, informative and factual; should also communicate annoyance and concern for the future.

## SAMPLE ANSWER: B

23 Ramblers Garden
Sandy Road
Donoghmane
Co. Leitrim
14/06/2013

Supt J. Maloney
Glencar Garda Station
Glencar
Co. Sligo

*[addressed properly]*

Dear Sir,

*[sincere tone]*

**It is with regret that** I write to you. It concerns the behaviour of our next door neighbours in 24 Ramblers Garden, Donoghmane, with whom you may be already familiar. We have resided at the above address for the best part of fifteen years and in that time we have never before been subjected to such **antisocial and disruptive behaviour**. Our neighbours, the Simonsons, have frequently been before the courts on various charges. This however, does not seem to have stopped their antisocial habits and disturbing traits. To use a cliché, these people are becoming the 'neighbours from hell'.

*[problem outlined]*

The older of the two men in the house, Mr David Simonson, repeatedly takes out power tools such as chainsaws and lawn mowers at all kinds of inappropriate times. The most recent of these incidents took place at **10.30pm on 29 May last**. His younger brother Rodney recently bought a new motorcycle and he regularly rides this vehicle around the small yard in our area at the most inappropriate times – often as late as two o'clock in the morning! There are regular party nights, when up to twenty colleagues gather there for the whole night. I have mentioned some of these incidents to you before; **the situation has since gone beyond what we can tolerate**.

*[factual information]* *[emotive sentence]*

There now also appears to be an incredible number of animals living with these men. My husband spotted a breed of large cat (perhaps a panther or small tiger) prancing around the green space at the rear of the building on 4 June last. Just last night we heard what sounded like a parrot or exotic bird squawking as if in pain; this noise continued for over forty minutes. This is alongside the seven or eight dogs already living in the house, some of which are downright vicious.

*[more practical information]*

To conclude, we feel that this situation cannot be tolerated any longer. **These people are a threat to the peace and stability of our small community**.

*[persuasive content]*

I appreciate the concern you have already shown regarding this issue and look forward to a response in the immediate future. My phone number is already on file with Garda Jim Doyle at the station.

**concluded properly** → Yours sincerely,

Teresa and Seamus O'Malley

(390 words approx.)

**EXAMINER'S ASSESSMENT**

- The layout of the letter is correct. Addresses, date, greeting and salutation are all in the appropriate format.
- The purpose is adhered to: the plight of a person living beside the 'neighbours from hell' is highlighted.
- The specifics of the disturbances are described well and remain factual throughout.
- The formal tone is appropriate for a formal letter of complaint to the authorities.
- Vocabulary is well chosen and not overly emotive. It is a long and detailed response worthy of a high grade.
- Marks: 15 (P) + 15 (C) + 15 (L) + 5 (M) = 50/50 (A1 grade).

## 3. Speeches and talks

These questions are for you if you can imagine yourself before an audience delivering a powerful speech or informative talk. If you have watched great **public speakers** such as politicians and leaders delivering speeches, copy their approach in your writing. Remember a time when you saw your school principal or another teacher give an **informative talk**. Perhaps you have experienced great team-talks given by **sports coaches** or mentors. Can you do the same in your writing?

In these answers, you are aiming to be both **informative** and **emotive**: you want people to understand you, but you also want them to **feel a certain way**.

This Question B appeared on the 2004 paper, accompanying the second comprehension piece.

## Question B
A Community Project in your Area:
Your community has been offered €100,000 for use on any local project. Write the speech that you would make to a meeting of the Local Community Association, in which you outline the project that you think the money should be spent on.

(50 marks)

This question can be broken down as follows:

**Task:** A speech to a local community association.

**Purpose:** Persuade the association that your idea is worth pursuing.

**Audience:** Members of the local community (male and female, young and old) who have an interest in local politics.

**Register:** Persuasive tone, outlining facts alongside emotive argument. Show a passionate commitment to improving the locality.

### SAMPLE ANSWER: B

[appropriately formal beginning] **Ladies and Gentlemen,**

It is a rare and wonderful time for us here in the community of Ballyfair. This welcome anonymous donation of €100,000 must be managed carefully. The donor made it very clear that it must be used for a non-profit-making purpose. Therefore, I fully believe that the choice of development is obvious to us all. It is time for Ballyfair to have its own community park and playground situated beside the former village green. **This has been suggested to me by numerous parents and residents. I speak on their behalf today**. [creates a sense of togetherness]

I remember growing up in this very village. **I remember the fun we had before the bulldozers and diggers realigned the main approach roads and the village centre**. We loved the freedom we had to play ball and chase each other around in safety. Many generations before us had done so too. [anecdotal]

[emotive phrase] **But the times changed rapidly; too rapidly in my opinion**. Now is the time to secure a new future for the next generation of youngsters. We will provide them with a modern, safe and well-equipped version of the old village green in the form of an enclosed park and playground facility, with all of the modern standards that our children and parents expect. I propose to build an environmentally sensitive play area, with swings and slides alongside plantings and hedging. There will be picnic tables and wooded shelters, framed by bark and sawdust surrounds – all of the highest standards. It will be the new focus of our beautiful and historic village. It will stand alongside and complement the new developments that now hold prominence in the village centre. It will also encourage more business for the single, struggling coffee shop here. People will now have an area to gather in peace in this new-found paradise.

Perhaps I am a bit over the top in suggesting that paradise is possible. But I **implore** all of you here to give this proposal a favourable consideration in light of this generous donation to our community. Make the right choice, people. **Build the park to build a better future for Ballyfair**.

Thank You.

*excellent vocabulary, mostly informative*

*very good verb*

*finishes with a political slogan*

(360 words approx.)

### EXAMINER'S ASSESSMENT

- The register here is excellent: the candidate blends **information** and **persuasion** very well. The tone is encouraging and pleading, without veering into begging or demanding.
- It is well structured. It references the past and the future, while debating the present.
- The vocabulary is very good. Clear enough for any audience to understand the points being made, without being too simplistic.
- An excellent answer overall.
- Marks: 15 (P) + 15 (C) + 15 (L) + 5 (M) = 50/50 (A1 grade).

## 4. Visual texts

Some students are more comfortable answering a question that is based upon a picture or a set of 'visuals' that appear on the exam paper. When analysing a visual, some basic points must be kept in mind:

### Context

The well-known 'w' questions apply here: **where, when, who, why** and **what**. They give us a sense of what the picture is about. Try to guess the context when you first look at the visual.

### Purpose

Context will go some way towards understanding the **purpose** of the visual. The picture has been taken for a reason. Guess what that reason might be.

## Point of view
From what angle do we see the picture? Is it close-up, long-distance, high-angle, low-angle, hidden, panoramic (seeing everything at once), etc?

## Framing
What is in the picture frame? Certain details are included and certain details are left out. Consider elements such as: background, foreground, left, right, centre, corners, middle, positioning, etc.

## Colour
Colour affects the way you feel about a picture.

- Bright colours such as yellows and oranges suggest happiness. Red can signify power, danger and adventure.
- Blue is the universal colour for calm. However, it can also suggest unhappiness ('the blues').
- Green is usually the colour for health and the environment. It is especially connected to Ireland and Irishness.
- Black and white visuals can suggest a particular atmosphere or capture a particular time. Remember context here: try to work out why the picture is in colour or black and white.
- Black and white visuals ask you to look more carefully at specific elements like shape and texture. They are also excellent for portraying facial expressions or capturing an event from the past.

The comprehension questions that accompany visual texts will ask you to **interpret or respond to what you see in the picture.** It may be useful for you to imagine being there at the moment the picture was captured. This allows for a huge variety of possible responses to the pictures. What is absolutely vital is that you **provide evidence for your view**. It does not matter if somebody sees it differently. What matters is **your way of explaining yourself.**

When responding to visual texts, **imagine being in the picture**.

You could follow the **statement–quotation–comment** approach that many teachers encourage in their classes:

- **State** what you see.
- **Quote** by mentioning specific details in the picture.
- **Comment** by backing up your view.

This question is taken from the 2005 paper: Comprehension Text 3, Question B.

## Question B

Imagine you were using one of the images in Text 3 to promote a particular holiday. Write a short advertisement to promote that holiday.

(50 marks)

Your answer is **inspired by** any **one** of the pictures. It should read like a radio script or a holiday brochure. **Information**, lots of **persuasion** and catchy **buzz words** are needed here. Deep analysis of the picture is not.

### SAMPLE ANSWER: B

*slogan*

**AIRBRAINS – THE AIRLINE WITH THE ANSWERS!**

*images of flying birds create sense of freedom*

You have seen the birds fly south for winter. Some even fly during the summer. Heck, **birds fly whenever they want**. The way this weather is lately, I bet you wish that you could, too. You may not have wings, but we at **Airbrains** will get them for you. For just €700 one-way, you can jet off with us on our **long-haul comfort planes** to **exotic southern destinations**. Cape Town, Rio de Janeiro, Singapore, Sydney and the Seychelles are all within reach with our excellently managed package deals. For an extra €55, you can find yourself in the natural wonders of New Zealand, where they say you can find '**four seasons in one day**'.

*company name*

*buzz words*

*cliché*

*tone of excitement*

For the true adventurer, we are now running our exclusive all-inclusive 15-day voyage to Antarctica, where **the sun shines 24 hours a day, even if it is still minus fourteen degrees!** Whatever your demands, we can put everything in place just to suit you. No more rain, misery and dreary Irish complaints about the state of the economy. **Follow that bird and follow that dream**. Airbrains is the unbeatable airline for long-haul holidays of a lifetime.

*persuasive language*

[margin note, left]: terms and conditions are almost an afterthought, often the case in advertising

**Terms and conditions apply**. Prices quoted are correct as of the beginning of April and cover the cost of flights to and from destinations only. Standard insurance does not cover frostbite in Antarctica. A full list of destinations is to be found at www.airbrains.cbs.com. **Log on for full details**.

[margin note, right]: makes the reader wonder if the advertisement is misleading; interesting touch

(240 words approx.)

### EXAMINER'S ASSESSMENT

- This is a fine answer that contains excellent, imaginative content based on Image 3 in the visuals.
- The catchy, humorous slogan draws in the reader successfully. It sets a tone that is somewhat satirical, but this is quite acceptable for this answer.
- The airline's name is memorable and the continued link with birds and flying is effective.
- Excellent use of alliteration throughout.
- Information appears throughout the piece. Interestingly, full details are available on the website only, as is the case in many real-life advertisements. The selling points appear to be the fine weather and adventure that are promised. We are unsure as to whether the trip would actually be great value for money.
- The 'terms and conditions' section is brilliant in the way that it evokes a realistic advertisement, hinting at some potentially questionable features of the product being advertised.
- While the answer is approximately 240 words only, it is nevertheless superb. It demonstrates the value of quality over quantity!
- Mark: 15 (P) + 15 (C) + 15 (L) + 5 (M) = 50/50 (A1 grade).

# Answer formats for B Questions

There is quite a variety in the B questions that could appear on your exam paper. Below are some pointers for different formats you might use in your answers:

## Newspaper articles

- **Read, read, read!** There is no substitute for reading newspapers regularly.
- **Tone**: When writing a newspaper article, decide immediately what the tone should be. Do you want it to be sincere, serious, light-hearted, sarcastic, angry, etc?
- **Headlines**: Tabloids tend to be more sensationalist than broadsheets, e.g. 'JAIL THE EVIL BEAST' as opposed to 'Killer to be sentenced tomorrow'. Tabloid headings can be very memorable. When Glasgow Celtic were beaten by Inverness Caledonian Thistle (a much smaller football team nicknamed 'Cally') the following headline appeared in a tabloid and reminded many people of *Mary Poppins*: 'SUPER-CALLY-GO-BALLISTIC-CELTIC-ARE-ATROCIOUS!!!'

- **Opening sentences**: All journalists are skilled at making an impact with their opening sentence.
- **Paragraph length**: Newspapers stick rigidly to one point per paragraph; words are not wasted.
- **Structure**: The most important information is placed at the start of the article. Lesser details are edited out or left to the end. This is called the 'upside-down pyramid' approach because readers frequently read only the start of an article.
- **Quotation**: Journalists use quotation carefully. When they are not sure of an exact quote, they paraphrase or use phrases like 'a source has indicated' or 'reports suggest that', etc.
- **Passive voice**: This means that an article should be written as if from a distance. The journalist does not let 'I' get in the way. They are not telling a story in the narrative sense; they report on what happened. For example: 'A bomb **was found** yesterday', rather than '**I heard** that there was a bomb'.

# Reports

- Similar to newspaper articles, reports must be **factual** and free from excessive emotion.
- You could be asked to report on a traffic accident, sports event, talent show, report to a committee at the end of the year, etc.
- The most important thing to consider when writing a report is your **audience**. Who are you reporting to?
- Reports must be very **informative**.

# Commentaries

- This question comes up occasionally. If you can copy the style of commentaries you hear on radio or TV, this is a possible choice.
- Commentaries require lots of emotion to communicate the excitement of an event. You will need to include some narration and information, but aesthetics should be your ultimate goal. Bring colour to the scene!
- Avoid cliché.
- Similar to tabloid newspaper headings, puns feature in commentaries:
  'It's snow joke: the race is being abandoned!'
  'It looks like curtains for Vladimir Karpets!'
  'John Carpenter nails his opponent!'
  'Woods is definitely in the trees!'
  'Keane to play no longer.'
  Try to include some funny puns in commentaries that you write.

## Advertising

- This is all about selling and the clever use of images (in your case, words) to encourage people to buy a product.
- Information and persuasion are on show here.
- An advertisement needs a **slogan**: a catchy phrase to gain attention. Sometimes slogans are funny or even shocking.
- **Memorable information**: Advertisements use scientific or technical language, but they keep it to a minimum.
- **Buzz words** include: 'best', 'unbeatable', 'superior' and 'a must'. Emotive sentences could be: 'Good parents always…'; 'Never, ever do…'; 'Could you possibly not…'; and 'You would be mad not to…'.
- **Repetition** is vital for product and brand recognition. Keep mentioning the product or the brand by name or by its benefit or result.

## Talks

- In many ways, this is the least formal of all the writing exercises in the exam.
- Once again, you must consider your audience.
- It is likely that this question will ask you to write a talk to be given to some of your **peers** or **colleagues**. Therefore, use the register (vocabulary, tone, purpose, etc.) that you would use when speaking to peers or friends. Practise this in class.
- When writing informal content, it is still important to avoid **slang** or phrases that are too casual, vague or loose. Avoid these phrases:

- like  • really  • kind of  • sort of  • yeah  • nah  • mate  • dude  • bud

*exam focus*

Choose the Comprehension B Question that you like most by determining the task involved and the type of writing that is required.

# 5 Composition

> **aims**
> - To analyse the **types of questions** that are found in the Composition section of the exam.
> - To demonstrate the key differences between **story** and **discussion** questions.
> - To understand the importance of **planning** in this section.

The Composition section accounts for 25 per cent of the entire exam.

This part of the exam will take you about **80 minutes** in total. You will not be writing all that time because choosing a title and writing a plan is of huge importance. Aim to write anything from **700 words upwards**. Some stories or speeches are likely to be longer. However, the old saying of '**quality not quantity**' applies here. Quality essay writing is dependent on good planning, so this aspect is covered in detail later on in this chapter.

25%

All writing can be broadly divided into two categories: **story** (narrative) or **discussion** (viewpoint, opinion or analysis). On occasion, good writing combines both: an informative newspaper article might include details of an event along with commentary or analysis. A really well-prepared student will include aspects of both if the question calls for it.

Breakdown of the Composition section:

- The paper contains **seven** composition titles.
- Students choose **one**: worth **100 marks** in total.
- Exam papers from the last number of years reveal that the titles given allow for a choice between a type of **story** and a type of **discussion**, or a combination of both.
- There is always an option to write a **personal essay** based on the visuals in the Comprehension section in Paper 1.

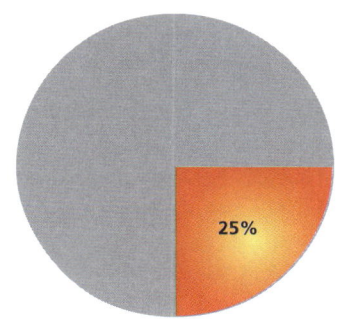

> **key point**
> If you want to write a talk, speech or article for your Composition, use the guidelines in Chapter 4 for Comprehension B Questions. However, remember that your **Composition answer must be longer**!

**Text 3**

*The Busker*

*The Charity Collectors – Daffodil Day*

*The Beggar and the Businessman*

*The Gambler*

Examine the following questions, taken from 2004, 2006 and 2008. The pattern is roughly the same each year. For each question, underline key words so that you are clear about the task at hand.

## 2004

Write a composition on **any one** of the following. Each composition carries 100 marks. The composition assignments below are intended to reflect language study in the areas of information, argument, persuasion, narration and the aesthetic use of language.

1. 'Twenty dollars a week doesn't go far.'

   Write an article for students giving them advice about making the most of the money they have. You may take a serious or a light-hearted approach. ← discussion

2. 'She had spent many a happy hour planning for something nice for him.'

   Write about an experience that showed you the importance of giving. You are free to write about any kind of giving. ← story/discussion

3. 'Suddenly she whirled from the window.'

   Write about a time when *you* acted on impulse. ← story

4. 'To dream better dreams.'

   Write a speech you would give to a group of young people in which you encourage them to follow their dreams. ← discussion

5. 'I wouldn't be comfortable in an 8,000 square foot home.'

   Write a personal account of what home means to you. ← discussion

6. 'Giving it all away.'

   Write a short story based on the idea of giving it all away. ← story

7. Write a narrative or short story based on any of the images in Text 3 (see above). ← story

## 2006

Write a composition on **any one** of the following. Each composition carries 100 marks. The composition assignments below are intended to reflect language study in the areas of information, argument, persuasion, narration and the aesthetic use of language.

**TEXT 3
THE HORROR INDUSTRY**

1. 'When I was small…'

    Tell about some of your best and worst experiences of being a young child. ◂ story

2. 'What a relief!'

    Write a short story ending with the above phrase. ◂ story

3. 'The big fears that most people share…'

    You are a newspaper reporter. Write about an important world event or issue which frightened people or worried them. ◂ story/discussion

4. 'We also spoke to a group of parents…'

    Write out the talk you would give to parents about your experience of being a teenager. ◂ story/discussion

5. 'Suddenly the evening changed…'

    Write about a time when you experienced change in your life. ◂ story

6. 'What is the fascination?'

    Write an account of some pastime or hobby that fascinates you. ◂ discussion

7. Write a short story based on one or more of the images in Text 3 (see above). ◂ story

## 2008

Write a composition on **any one** of the following. Each composition carries 100 marks. The composition assignments below are intended to reflect language study in the areas of information, argument, persuasion, narration and the aesthetic use of language.

1. 'He had no choice.'
   Write a short story which contains the above phrase. *[story]*

2. 'It's called Paradise.'
   Write a personal account of your idea of paradise. *[story/discussion]*

3. 'Breaking down barriers.'
   Write an article for a school magazine in which you make suggestions to students on how to welcome newcomers into the school community. *[story/discussion]*

4. 'Robot servants or "house-bots" in our homes.'
   Write a short story based on this idea. *[story]*

5. 'A special friend.'
   Write a personal account of what friendship means to you. *[story/discussion]*

6. 'Grab life with both hands.'
   Write the speech you would give to a group of young people on the importance of having a positive attitude towards life. *[discussion]*

7. Write a narrative or short story based on one of the images in Text 3 (see above). *[story]*

### Text 3

**PICTURES OF IRISH LIFESTYLE 2008**

1. **A special friend from a different world**
   Shot on the west coast of Ireland, as a dolphin takes more interest in the swimmer, rather than the other way round.

2. **The Spire, O'Connell St., Dublin**
   A wonderful new take on a well known landmark.

3. **A well earned break**
   A young girl taking a well earned break while clearing up leaves.

4. **Model goalie gives it extra**
   The solitude and determination of a camogie player as she strikes the ball with what seems like a perfect swing.

5. **It's in the net**
   Rock pools are still a source of fascination to children.

6. **Grab life with both hands**
   A relationship between man and boy on Ireland's south east coast, as they stride to avoid the incoming tide.

Once you have chosen your question, you will most likely be writing one of the following types of composition:

- Short story.
- Personal essay: A story or discussion based on your own experience. The 'I' voice is important here.
- Talk or speech to an audience.
- An article of some sort, e.g. newspaper, magazine, blog, etc.

Spend some time **browsing** these and other essay titles. Make a note of the titles you would prefer and those you would avoid prefer to avoid. This is the first step in choosing a title and properly planning your essays.

The Composition question is sometimes referred to as the 'essay question'. Some students are intimidated by the thoughts of writing such an essay. It may indeed be the longest piece of continuous writing you have ever written.

> **key point**
> It is a serious error in the exam to choose a story or a personal experience essay if that is not where your strengths lie.

Over the years, some preconceived notions about the Composition question have taken hold. Let's tackle them here:

1. **'The essay can be made up off the top of your head on the day.'**
   *False*

   A certain amount of imagination and creativity is required to do the composition. However, the student who thinks that the perfect essay will just land from space at the right moment is deluded. You must focus very clearly on what the question asks of you. For example, the **marking scheme for a short story is very specific** about what is expected:

   ### Marking scheme for a short story
   The writing will be shaped as a story, i.e. – have a sense of a beginning, middle and end; a defined setting somewhere in time; have a character, one usually confronted by a problem or obstacle; have some sense of a time-line incorporating a defining moment (tension, climax, resolution) … etc.

   It is obvious that planning and practice before the exam is vital.

2. **'Writing a story is always the best option.'**
   *False*

   This issue is of huge significance. While it may seem easy to write a story, other options such as a speech, magazine article or personal essay may suit certain candidates better. If you are not a good storyteller, you will still have plenty of options on the day.

   It is important that you work with your teacher to determine if you have adequate storytelling skills. Otherwise, avoid the short story options and concentrate on something else. Look back over some Junior Certificate short stories and see if they inspire you to write your own story.

3. **'The essay will decide if you get an A grade or not, or if the examiner will pass or fail you.'**
   *Partly True*

   Given that this question comprises 25 per cent of the entire exam, it does have a major bearing on your overall grade. However, it is marked according to strict criteria and examiners are trained to look for particular qualities and features. They are not out to judge your opinions or views; they need to examine your language skills.

4. **'Personal, unique, original essays get automatic A grades.'**
   *False*

   Perhaps you have heard of some famous A1 essays. Like the one entitled 'Creation', where a candidate drew a map of the world. Or an essay entitled 'Why?', for which the candidate wrote 'Why not?'. Or best of all, the one about 'Bravery', which inspired a bright student to hand up four blank pages. What grade did they all receive? Such efforts obviously get zero! A good student will aim for anything from **700 words upwards**, which amounts to roughly **two and a half or three A4 pages as a bare minimum.**

5. **'You can learn off an essay and twist it to suit any exercise.'**
   *Possible – But not at all advisable*

   Some teachers and those who give grinds have suggested this approach. It is fraught with danger, not least the possibility that the student will fail to answer the question asked, which is one of the main reasons for poor grades in English. 'Learned-off' essays that are unoriginal do not score well. You can, of course, use an essay plan or outline that went well for you during the year, provided that you follow what the essay question asks of you in the actual exam.

6. **'The Composition is the most important question of the entire exam.'**
   *Partly True*

   Again, with 25 per cent on the line, this is an area to which students must devote time and practice. It is also worth reminding you that no amount of practice and preparation can account for simply writing a bad essay on the day. However, if you make some good choices and write to your full potential, you should be fine.

   **key point**
   It's all in the plan!

# Option 1: A short story

## Planning

As rugby pundit George Hook once said, rule number one for making chicken soup is to catch the chicken! The same applies to writing a short story composition. Catch the chicken by making a **sensible, coherent plan**:

- **Underline key words and jot down ideas.** This applies to all questions on the paper, but the composition is mostly about **your own ideas and expression,** so try to think broadly about the topic once you have underlined the key words.
- **Spend at least 15 minutes planning the detail.** All planning begins with **brainstorming.** It can take the form of spider diagrams or mind maps – whatever way you can comfortably get your thoughts on the page. You may scribble single words or draw diagrams; it really does not matter once you have a way of doing it. Then connect the ideas by following the pointers below.
- The **narrative voice** of a story is important. Pick one of these options:
    1. I am in the story, telling it. This is a **first person narrative**.
    2. I am outside the story, telling it. An 'all-seeing' narrator is used in **third person narrative**.

> **exam focus**
> Remember that first person narratives don't have to be true to life. Invent a story about yourself. You can be anybody!

## Key ingredients for a good short story

- Have a **small number of characters**: two or three characters with one main character or **protagonist.** When planning, create a quick profile of each character, listing gender, age, features, etc.
- Give each personality **one strong trait**, such as: aggression; impatience; humour; an unusual talent; unique features, etc.
- Work within a **narrow timeframe**. The hub of your story could take place in a few hours or one single day, with a significant episode.
- Include **dialogue** and interaction. Use these elements to suggest details to the reader, e.g. the setting, time and location.
- In order to interest your reader, there must be a challenge, obstacle or **conflict** that the main character must overcome. All good stories contain conflict.
- There must be **tension** or uncertainty before your conflict is resolved. Situations in real life rarely run smoothly; when they do, they make for boring stories.
- Know the **ending** before you begin.
- Understand the purpose of stories. Aim to entertain and **engage** the reader. If the story bores you, it will bore the reader, too.
- Remember the **audience** for your story. In this case, it will be the examiner.
- Do not be at all inhibited or shy about expressing yourself. Speak from the well of your own experiences. Be creative!

## Bad planning

To demonstrate how things can go wrong without a plan, read the following passage from a student who chose Question 2 from the 2006 exam. It asks for a short story ending with the sentence: 'What a relief!' The student wrote the entire essay without any planning. So many problems are demonstrated in just this opening paragraph. See if you can identify these weaknesses yourself before reading the analysis overleaf.

> **What a relief!**
>
> Five best friends spent months planning their dream vacation trying to find the perfect place with a mixture of nights out, a relaxing atmosphere during the day and a place you would only go once in a lifetime. John was a typical teenager and loved nothing more than going out with his friends. He was tall and strong and a gym fanatic. He was nineteen years old. John's four best friends were the same age as him and they were friends since playschool. Despite what most people thought, John's friends were not as bad as they seemed. They were party animals and always went out any chance they had, drinking and taking as much drugs as they could get into them. They decided to go to Bangkok in Thailand for six weeks.

## Analysis of sample paragraph

This opening paragraph reads like an essay disaster waiting to happen.

- In a short story, you have little time to develop characters. Choose two or three at most. This student has included **far too many characters** for a short story composition.
- Try to avoid **common names** like John or Mary. Go for something more memorable.
- **Personalities** are important. Why does John have to be a 'typical teenager'? Surely it is more interesting to read about a character that is unusual or unique. Also, few nineteen-year-olds fit the bill as 'typical teenagers'.
- Timeframe is crucial. This paragraph suggests that the action will cover a total of six weeks. This is **far too long a timeframe** for this kind of composition. It is better to write short episodes covering a day in the life – even a few minutes in the lives – of a small number of characters.
- The **content** is rather clichéd. The story of five young males heading to Thailand for six weeks has been told so many times. Given the title, it is quite likely that the boys will: have a brush with the law; dabble in drink, drugs, sex or a combination of them all; and somehow escape with their lives to exclaim 'What a Relief!' This storyline is unoriginal, predictable and lacks imagination. If it was a film, you wouldn't bother watching it.
- Other storylines that are overdone include:
  - Scoring the winning goal in a football final.
  - Waking up to discover that 'it was all a dream'.
  - Describing complicated intimate relationships between boyfriends and girlfriends.
  - Killing off the narrator at the end. This seldom makes sense in the context of a story.
  - Any type of clichéd, overused storylines involving: drinking, drugs, parties, pregnancies, the police, etc.

While there might be some merit in these subject areas, the problem is that they tend not to be very interesting or **original**. Examiners feel that they have heard all of these stories before and so they will not score them highly in the exam. Therefore, **don't write about them**, unless the question specifically asks you to.

- Given the title, the ending for this story is of huge importance. In fact, **the ending is crucial in all stories** and students should know the end before they begin to write. This title suggests a happy ending: John probably escapes with his life. But perhaps the final phrase could be the words of the police-chief in Thailand who is delighted to put John behind bars for his drug-trafficking crimes. It is up to you to determine the ending. Just make sure you decide on it before you begin to write.

- We have examined the **content** problems with this sample paragraph. However, there are also **style** issues to be considered. **How** the story is written (vocabulary, sentence structure, grammar, etc.) accounts for another 40 per cent of the marks. Clearly there are style problems in this sample paragraph also: the **opening sentence** is too long; the **vocabulary** is limited; and overall there is not much to recommend it.

> **exam focus**: Include any rough work or planning you did with your answer booklet. Examiners do take note of this material.

> **key point**: The opening paragraph is the most important paragraph to get right.

## Improving your effort

Let's look at Question 1 from the 2008 paper. It's a straightforward title that provides lots of imaginative potential: 'He had no choice.'

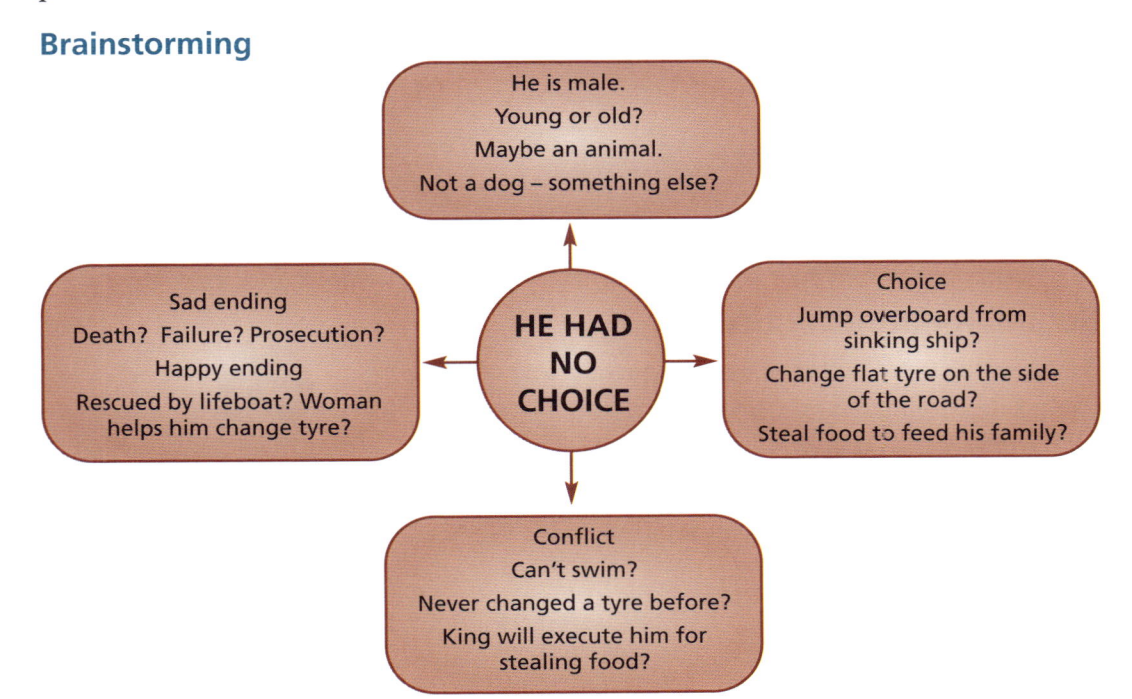

### Brainstorming

**HE HAD NO CHOICE**

- He is male. Young or old? Maybe an animal. Not a dog – something else?
- Choice: Jump overboard from sinking ship? Change flat tyre on the side of the road? Steal food to feed his family?
- Conflict: Can't swim? Never changed a tyre before? King will execute him for stealing food?
- Sad ending: Death? Failure? Prosecution? Happy ending: Rescued by lifeboat? Woman helps him change tyre?

Looking at this brainstorm, the storyline with most potential is one involving one male character (the protagonist) who needs to change a tyre but can't. It is a simple, familiar scenario, so it needs a twist. Here are some options:

- He discovers some money by the side of the road and a story involving drug dealers and criminals follows. This seems overly complicated and not very plausible.
- He is murdered by a psychopath on the loose from an institution. This seems silly and far-fetched.
- He phones a friend who rescues him. This is a happy ending but it lacks any real tension or excitement.
- **He is rescued by a helpful woman and the story ends happily.**

The final suggestion has the most potential. It would work best because:

- This storyline is a little **unusual**, but not entirely **unlikely**.
- It has just **two characters**, who deal with an incident that takes place **one evening**.
- There is a **conflict** or problem to overcome, with some uncertainty as to whether it will be solved.
- The hero in this case is a **heroine**. In an **original** way, it is the woman who comes to the rescue of the stricken young man.
- **Who is the woman?** That is up to you to decide!

Now that we have the ingredients for a good short story, let's think about **structure**. Stories will have:

- A beginning/introduction.
- A middle section/main body.
- An ending/conclusion.

## Beginning/Introduction

The opening is probably the most important part of all compositions. Practise opening paragraphs.

It is important to **set the scene.** Don't list factual details; instead, hint at the time and place in which the story is set. Show what is happening; don't just tell.

**key point**

The golden rule for all narratives is: **show, don't tell.**

## SHOW, DON'T TELL

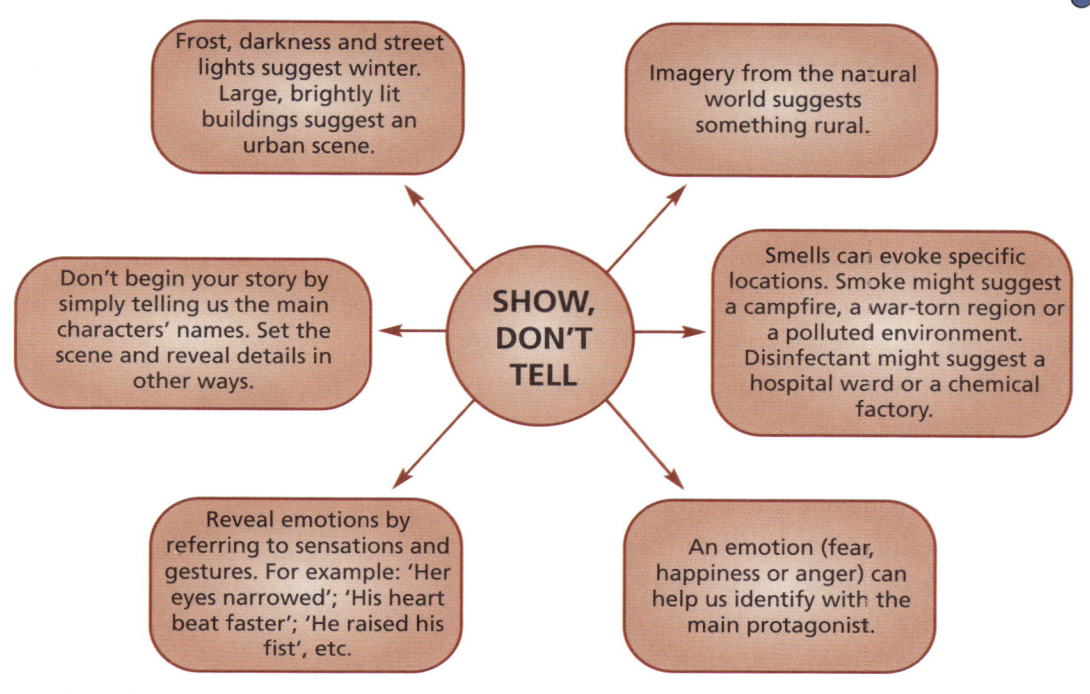

- Frost, darkness and street lights suggest winter. Large, brightly lit buildings suggest an urban scene.
- Imagery from the natural world suggests something rural.
- Don't begin your story by simply telling us the main characters' names. Set the scene and reveal details in other ways.
- Smells can evoke specific locations. Smoke might suggest a campfire, a war-torn region or a polluted environment. Disinfectant might suggest a hospital ward or a chemical factory.
- Reveal emotions by referring to sensations and gestures. For example: 'Her eyes narrowed'; 'His heart beat faster'; 'He raised his fist', etc.
- An emotion (fear, happiness or anger) can help us identify with the main protagonist.

Look at the opening paragraph below:

> It hadn't rained for two weeks. The weathermen were sure that the high pressure would keep the southern coast dry for another while, maybe even up to Christmas. But keeping track of the weather in this part of the island was a very tricky job. People had a tendency to take each day as it came, knowing how changeable things could be and how wrong the reports had been before.

We can tell from this opening paragraph that it is winter in a place where weather is changeable and where people appear close to nature and an outdoor life. It seems rural (being an island) and there is a nervous sense about the place. This story has endless possibilities at this point.

## Middle section/Main body

Given the time constraints in the exam, it is best to immediately engage the reader with the main protagonist. Introduce a character early on. Identify some strong trait(s). Show how the character is faced with a conflict or dilemma.

> Not so with Brendan. Weather, fishermen, holidays and Christmas were far from his mind now. All he cared about was his new Honda Civic, imported from the mainland on a cheap deal and now the love of his life. So what if it

> wasn't exactly a sports car or a top-of-the-range coupe? He had wheels, and a twenty-one-year-old with wheels could have girls. Not those brainless local girls he wasted his time with before; real women this time.

Important information has been revealed: the character's name is Brendan and his strong trait seems to be confidence. However, we wonder if it is genuine confidence.

A good story will now present an obstacle or **problem** that will challenge Brendan's confidence. This creates **conflict**. What options are there?

- We will avoid the boy-racer stereotype. It is too predictable.
- We could suggest that Brendan is a shy and insecure type of young man; his confidence is a mask.
- One possibility is that Brendan's car gets a flat tyre. Because of this, we learn that he actually knows nothing about cars and has no idea how to change the tyre. This could become the obstacle or conflict in the story.
- Imagine Brendan stranded as dusk comes. He seems helpless. Then a car stops. Brendan wonders who it might be. We reach the key moment of the story, where **tension** is at its highest.

**key point**
Practice makes perfect! Try writing your own sample paragraphs for this scenario.

> He did not recognise the car immediately. The sun had long disappeared below the horizon. The engine cut. He then realised that he didn't know too many other islanders' cars either. Maybe it was a tourist? But why a tourist would be in this back-of-beyond place right now wasn't interesting Brendan. The window rolled down with a squeak. Brendan leaned forward anxiously. Whether it would be an axe murderer or a good Samaritan, he had no idea. Either way, he needed help badly.

What follows has a huge bearing on the end or **resolution** of the story. It is an unexpected twist, but a pleasant one.

> A vaguely familiar voice called out: 'This is no place to be stuck on a night like this. What's up?' Brendan couldn't believe it. He just about managed an answer.
> 'Eh … just out for a quick spin round. Didn't get too far, got a puncture, just about to change it. Do you have a phone I can borrow? Where are you going yourself?'
> It was the first time Brendan had spoken to Mrs Wilson, his primary school principal, in nearly ten years. Having tormented him for most of his youth, she was the last person he needed to see right now. But as the saying goes, any port in a storm.

Now we have a story with two characters meeting in unusual circumstances, which provide an opportunity for them to patch up some past difficulties as they help each other out in a crisis.

Notice how this section introduces the other character. It doesn't just tell us who she is; she is revealed through the clever use of dialogue. Again, the writer is showing **rather than telling** the reader.

## Ending/Conclusion

> Brendan slowly edged out from the side of the road, deliberately waiting for Mrs Wilson to drive away in her husband's Volvo. 'There are obvious benefits to being married to a garage owner,' she reminded him. She may have failed in her valiant attempts to civilise him with doses of long division and the teachings of the Bible. But at least she demonstrated the hugely valuable skill of changing a tyre on a Honda Civic. 'I'll get myself some real women, alright.' It wasn't exactly what he had in mind earlier that evening.
>
> THE END

This conclusion links with our first meeting of Brendan. We see his shyness, insecurity and mask of confidence. The final paragraph brings the story to a conclusion. It is a happy resolution, although it may not have been expected. This short story would score well in the exam, mostly because it is well planned and follows a clear outline.

**key point: Understand the structure of a good short story.**

# Option 2: A personal essay

The personal essay asks you to write about an experience you had. Thankfully, it involves **planning** that is broadly similar to the short story. The main difference is that it is expected to be more **sincere** than an imaginative story. This means that you write from what the marking scheme calls the **'engaged "I" persona'**. You can mix real-life experiences with reactions and heartfelt opinions following on from experiences you have had.

You must be wary of some **common pitfalls**. Students sometimes write about experiences that are simply not very interesting. Or sometimes they express an opinion that is not thought out fully or is badly informed, in spite of their personal experiences. Examples of themes that are often dealt with poorly include: racism, world politics and relationships.

## Improving the personal essay option

You should follow all of the advice given for planning a story. When you read an essay title, ask yourself if you have knowledge or experience of it. Do you hold strong opinions on the topic? If you are unsure, don't choose this particular essay title.

In 2008, one of the essay options asked students for their **personal idea of paradise**. Many students were attracted to this title. In a sense, paradise can be whatever or wherever you want it to be. But it would help your essay greatly if you had been somewhere that felt like paradise or if you had a strong idea or an opinion of such a place. Use your own feelings, experiences and opinions as much as you can when writing the personal essay.

> **exam focus**
> Identify the **idea** or concept suggested in each personal essay title. If you don't know enough about the concept, don't do this essay!

Being clear about **purpose**, **audience** and **register** (**PAR**) is an essential skill for doing Paper 1. It is particularly important when it comes to the personal essay question.

> **key point**
> Check past exam papers and study the visuals, which usually accompany Comprehension Text 3. **Practise short paragraphs** inspired by these visuals.

## Purpose

Ask yourself what your essay aims to achieve. If you intend to describe paradise, your essay must be one that would genuinely appeal to any reader. It must be convincing. You will have to include the **language of persuasion**, along with some **narration** and **aesthetics.**

## Audience

Consider who you are writing the essay for. Obviously the examiner will read your essay, but you should write with the presumption that it could be read and appreciated by others. Therefore, you should imagine that you are writing for someone you can trust. Think of your reader as someone who won't judge you, but is **interested in hearing you say something interesting**.

## Register

Remember that register involves many elements. It requires: specific **vocabulary**; appropriate **tone**; and proper **treatment of the task** at hand.

It is helpful to fill out a **PAR plan** before you write a personal essay. Examine the plan for 'My Idea of Paradise' below.

| My Idea of Paradise | | |
|---|---|---|
| **Purpose** | **Audience** | **Register** |
| • To show that I have a clear idea of the concept: paradise.<br>• To describe clearly my version of paradise. | • Friends who would understand me.<br>• People who would not ridicule my view, but ask questions about it.<br>• The examiner, who will grade my effort. | • Sincere: it needs to sound like I really mean it.<br>• Light-hearted: since it is a pleasant topic.<br>• Convincing: I need to explain myself well and convince the examiner of my point of view. |

## Personal essay based on visuals (Pictures)

If you decide to write a personal essay in response to the visuals on your exam paper, be very sure about your choice. You will be required to write a **full-length essay** for your answer. Sometimes students run out of things to say about the visuals after a page or two and this makes for a poor personal essay.

A personal essay based on visuals can be a last resort for a student desperate to write something in the exam. On the other hand, it could be the first choice for many students. Some students like to learn things visually and they can easily respond to pictures. If you **like reading visual texts**, then a personal essay based on visuals might be the perfect choice for you.

# Clarity and coherence

The Composition section is a tremendous test of your vocabulary and expression. There are many tips and language aids available for this question. However, the most important thing to remember is the need for **clarity and coherence**:

- Have **clear ideas** in your head. Think before you write!
- Write **coherent sentences**. This means keeping things simple and understandable.

You cannot go far wrong if you keep these things in mind.

## Sentences

Below is some useful information about sentences:

- Each sentence must have a **subject**, i.e. something doing the action.
  Example: The Shannon is the longest river in Ireland.
- Each sentence must have a **verb**, i.e. the action word.
  Example: The Shannon flows through the midlands.
- Each sentence must be a **complete thought**.
- If one or more of these elements is missing, then you have a **phrase**, rather than a sentence.
  Examples:   – flows through the midlands (no subject)
  – longest river in Ireland (no subject or verb)
- Using phrases rather than complete sentences can lead to lower quality writing. Always ensure your sentences contain: a subject, a verb and a complete thought.
- Sentences can become more complex, but if you **read** and **write** a lot you will gain confidence in structuring them.

## Improving your expression

A **dictionary** or **thesaurus** can be very useful in improving your expression and adding depth to your sentences. Here is an example of a simple sentence:

*The Shannon flows through the midlands.*

This is a basic sentence using informative language. See how it changes when we add some **adjectives**. Adjectives are descriptive words used to modify nouns.

*The **majestic, sparkling** Shannon flows through the **lush, flat** midland region of Ireland.*

We can also include **adverbs**. Adverbs are descriptive words used to modify verbs.

*The majestic, sparking Shannon flows **lazily** through the lust, flat midland region of Ireland.*

We can even add new **phrases** or **clauses**:

*The majestic, sparkling Shannon, **Ireland's longest river,** flows lazily through the lush, flat midland region of the country.*

Notice how the extra clause is added; it is separated with commas. See how the end of the sentence is tweaked to avoid repetition. 'Region of Ireland' has become 'region of the country' to avoid repetition of the word 'Ireland'.

## Paragraphs

A paragraph contains a series of sentences that are linked by the same theme or idea. Here are some tips on using paragraphs:

- Become comfortable with paragraphs by practising your essays regularly. All good compositions are paragraphed well.
- Start a new paragraph when you want to move to: a new point; a new location; a new idea; a new speaker; new dialogue; or when you want to conclude your essay.
- Paragraphs are strongly advised in exam answers because they show that you have put order and structure on your work.
- Even if you are not entirely certain, begin a new paragraph if you feel you should. Paragraphs always look better on the page than a big, solid block of text.

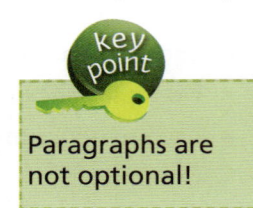

> **key point**
> Paragraphs are not optional!

## Tips for avoiding some common pitfalls

- Aim for the *right* word, rather than a big word that you may not be able to use correctly.
- Regularly read a **thesaurus** so that your vocabulary is not narrow.
- Verbs, adjectives and adverbs should be varied as much as possible to breathe life and colour into your work.
- Avoid starting too many sentences with 'I'. While engagement with the task is vital, the composition is not really all about you. Try to think outside of yourself in order to be creative.
- Not everybody is as funny as they think they are. Writing good comedy is generally regarded as very challenging. Only do it if you know you are good at it and it is a suitable occasion.

- Don't shoot yourself in the foot by apologising for not knowing things. Be decisive and confident in yourself. This will come across in your writing.

## Meaningless words

'Verbiage' is a great word for what is also called waffle! This occurs when we include unnecessary words or when we use words that carry little or no meaning. Look at some examples below:

| | |
|---|---|
| Smile *on his face* | (Where else would it be?) |
| Few *in number* | (Few already indicates a number.) |
| *Past* history | (History is in the past.) |
| *Very* unique | (Unique means one of a kind. There is no such thing as 'very unique'.) |
| Rectangular *shape* | (A rectangle is a shape.) |
| Meet *together* | ('Meet' means coming together.) |
| Small *in size* | ('Small' indicates size.) |
| *General* public | (Is there a non-general public?) |

If you read quality newspapers and books, you will avoid verbiage and you will understand and appreciate good writing.

## Words and expressions to be avoided!

The following expressions do not exist:
- Could of
- Would of
- Might of
- Should of
- Alot

The following expressions do exist, but they are used far too often!
- Sort of
- You know
- Like

**Key point:** If you use coarse or vulgar language in your Leaving Certificate exam, your final grade will be seriously affected.

## Emphatic words

When you use too many emphatic words, you imply that what you're saying is absolute fact and is not open to argument.

The following emphatic words should be used carefully:
- Always
- Never
- All
- None
- Total
- Complete
- Absolute
- Entire

## Hyperbole

Hyperbole is pronounced 'hi-per-boh-lay' and means gross exaggeration. To describe Yeats as the 'greatest, most outstanding, supreme poet in any language whatsoever' might fit your beliefs, but it would be more measured to say: 'I admire Yeats for the following reasons...'

## Clichés

Try to avoid clichéd phrases. Use the table below to improve your writing. On the left are some particularly clichéd phrases. Think of original ways of expressing these same ideas and write your new phrases on the right.

| | |
|---|---|
| A game of two halves | |
| Raining cats and dogs | |
| Daylight robbery | |
| Pure class | |
| Going forward | |
| In the current climate | |
| The writing is on the wall | |
| As black as coal | |
| As cold as ice | |
| As red as blood | |
| As blue as the sea | |
| As dark as night | |
| As white as snow | |
| At the end of the day | |
| Backs to the wall | |
| In this day and age | |
| Ordinary man in the street | |
| Leave no stone unturned | |
| Openness and transparency | |
| Cool, calm and collected | |
| To be sure | |
| A terrible tragedy | |
| Sight for sore eyes | |
| Knee high to a grasshopper | |
| Coming on leaps and bounds | |

You might have to use clichés on occasion and the examiner might not penalise you too much for them. However, the whole idea of the exam is to test your expression. So think creatively and aim for originality!

# Paper 2

## 6 The Single Text

**aims**
- To analyse the **typical questions** that accompany the Single Text section.
- To outline **key areas for revision** of the Single Text.
- To see the **overlap between Paper 1 revision and revision for the Single Text**.

The Single Text section accounts for 15 per cent of the entire exam.

You will have studied **one text in great detail** for this part of the exam. As a result, the questions will be quite specific in this section.

### Single Texts for 2014
*Pride and Prejudice* (Austen)
*Circle of Friends* (Binchy)
*Empire of the Sun* (Ballard)
*Translations* (Friel)
*Never Let Me Go* (Ishiguro)
*How Many Miles to Babylon?* (Johnston)
*Sive* (Keane)
*Home Before Night* (Leonard)
*Macbeth* (Shakespeare)

### Single Texts for 2015
*Pride and Prejudice* (Austen)
*Circle of Friends* (Binchy)
*How Many Miles to Babylon?* (Johnston)
*The Great Gatsby* (Fitzgerald)
*Never Let Me Go* (Ishiguro)
*Home Before Night* (Leonard)
*All My Sons* (Miller)
*Juno and the Paycock* (O'Casey)
*Othello* (Shakespeare)

**exam focus**
On the day of the exam, there will be quite a number of pages of Paper 2 that are of no relevance to you. So, **quickly identify your Single Text questions** and ignore ones that aren't for you!

## Allocation of marks

There are 60 marks available for this section. The marks are divided as follows:
- There are **three 10-mark questions**, which focus on a **key moment** or some **key characters** and your reaction or **opinion**. **Do all three of the 10-mark questions.**
- There are **three 30-mark questions**, which require longer answers. **Choose ONE 30-mark question.**

## Essential items for revision

There are some absolute essentials for revision of the Single Text. Concentrate on the following elements and you should have enough material to begin revising for any question.
1. Key characters: their behaviour and traits.
2. Setting: the place and time of the text.
3. Main themes: the essential points/issues of the text.

### 1. Key characters: Their behaviour and traits

A look at any selection of past papers will show that a detailed knowledge of the **key characters** and **key events** in a text will enable you to answer most questions on the day.

#### Step 1
Begin by **listing the key characters** in your chosen text. Three or four may be enough. If your text is Shakespearean, however, the list may be longer in order to include secondary characters.

Example: Key characters in *Macbeth*
- Macbeth.
- Lady Macbeth.
- Banquo.
- Macduff.
- The Three Witches.

#### Step 2
Next, make a list of **adjectives** you would use to **describe each character**. Look at the example of Lady Macbeth and continue this task for every character in your text.

> **LADY MACBETH**
> Evil
> Manipulative
> Deceptive
> Assertive
> Defeated

## Step 3

Now think about the **key events**. These could include scenes in a play or key moments in a novel. **In order to score high points, you should know significant quotes from each of the key events in the text.**

Look at these significant quotes from some key events involving Lady Macbeth:

> Act 1, Scene 5, 38–43
> 'The raven himself is hoarse
> That croaks the fatal entrance of Duncan
> Under my battlements. Come, you spirits
> That tend on mortal thoughts, unsex me here,
> And fill me from the crown to the toe topful
> Of direst cruelty'

> Act 1, Scene 5, 74–5
> 'Look like the innocent flower, but be the serpent under't'

> Act 1, Scene 7, 60–1
> 'But screw your courage to the sticking place,
> And we'll not fail.'

> Act 3, Scene 4, 65–8
> 'Sit, worthy friends; my lord is often thus,
> And hath been from his youth. Pray you, keep seat.
> The fit is momentary; upon a thought
> He will again be well.'

> Act 5, Scene 1, 36–7
> 'Out, damn'd spot! out, I say!—One; two: why, then
> 'tis time to do't.—Hell is murky.

## Step 4

**Bring it all together. Use your notes to construct small paragraphs – or even simple sentences to begin with.**

- When we first encounter Lady Macbeth in Act 1, she communicates a deep-rooted sense of evil. She calls on spirits to 'unsex' her so that she is full of 'direst cruelty'. She is asking to be less feminine and to have the determination to carry out dreadful deeds, the worst of which is the killing of the King.

- Lady Macbeth uses the imagery of the flower and the serpent to explain how true intentions can be cloaked.
- Lady Macbeth easily manipulates her husband. By questioning his courage, she questions his value as a man, soldier and faithful husband.
- In the banquet scene, it is Lady Macbeth who holds things together as her husband is overwhelmed by the presence of Banquo's ghost.
- Lady Macbeth's constant washing of her hands and references to spots of blood is a sign that she is now overcome with the weight of guilt caused by her descent into evil. By this time it is too late and she dies off stage, most likely by suicide.

Follow this four-step process in revising the characters in your Single Text.

## 2. Setting: Place and time

Where and when a text is set is of enormous significance. Each text has a background or **social setting** that should allow us to understand the **behaviour** and **motivations** of characters and **why events turn out the way they do**.

When revising your Single Text, think about its setting. **List the words that best capture the place and time associated with your text.** Consider the **values** that were important in this setting. This will say a lot about how the characters see the world and how they react to their circumstances.

Let's take the example of John B. Keane's *Sive*.

**SETTING**
- Rural Kerry, south-west Ireland.
- Late 1950s.
- Agriculture is the dominant industry.
- Poverty is widespread.
- Catholic values are rigidly enforced.
- Life is an ongoing struggle.

Adjectives that capture the sense of **PLACE**
- Insular.
- Remote.
- Harsh.
- Cold and wet.

- Uncompromising.
- Colourful.
- Tense.
- Depressing.

Adjectives that capture the dominant **VALUES**
- Greedy.
- Frustrated.
- Bitter.
- Jealous.
- Lonely.
- Ambitious.
- Catholic.
- Loving.

Once you have made these lists, you will have the raw material you need in order to construct short, basic practice paragraphs that will help you to answer the questions that appear on the exam paper.

## 3. Themes

All texts involve **themes** or issues that the writer wants to address. Once we have finished the text, we should know what the main point of the text is, i.e. what important questions and issues are addressed in the text. Writers want to challenge the way we think. Therefore, when revising your Single Text, begin by **jotting down the main issues or themes that you found** while studying it. This is an important starting point.

Then, it becomes important to **develop these short notes** into more detailed responses. If you consider the main theme of *How Many Miles to Babylon?* by Jennifer Johnston, you could proceed as follows:

1. **A basic answer:**
   War.

2. **A better answer:**
   How war affects people in different ways, e.g. the different attitudes of Alec and Major Glendinning.

3. **A well-developed opening paragraph:**

The horrors of war and the ways in which warfare can affect our attitudes are the major themes of *How Many Miles to Babylon?* The friendship that was so precious to Alec and Jerry growing up is changed forever by their fate in the trenches. Alec's mercy killing of his friend at the novel's conclusion, as well as his own execution, is a bleak and depressing end to this sad tale. The brutality of the war has left us disturbed. We are reminded that in war there are no happy endings. This is the issue at the centre of Jennifer Johnston's novel.

We can see how a basic answer can be fleshed out into a good paragraph that explains the important theme of the text. There are only six sentences in the paragraph, but it is still a high-standard response.

This 'snippet' approach of writing short paragraphs is much more practical than writing numerous long essays in the run up to the exam. You will have to answer whatever questions appear on the exam paper on the day. If you prepare and revise enough of these short paragraphs in advance, you can adapt them on the day to fit with whatever questions come up. This is much better than learning long, essay-style answers that can't be adapted.

**exam focus**

Practise writing **short, precise paragraphs** that can be used in both 10-mark and 30-mark questions.

**exam Q**

Below are sample questions and answers that demonstrate different levels of answering on 10-mark and 30-mark questions. Remember to stick to the statement–quotation–comment approach: if you make a point, you must quote and support it with evidence from the text.

**10-MARK QUESTIONS**

Typical questions include:
- Describe what happens when…
- How does [an event] occur?
- Write a short account of…

## THE SINGLE TEXT

- Why do you think [an event] happened?
- Choose your favourite moment and explain your choice.
- How would you react if...?
- Which character do you prefer in the scene where...?
- What was the most dramatic, amusing or interesting scene or character?

**key point**

1. Make a **statement** that addresses the question.
2. Include **quotation** that properly refers to the text.
3. Provide **commentary** that backs up the point you made.

If you follow this format and write approximately 100 words each time, you will be on your way to a good grade.

### Below is a 10-mark question about character.

*Macbeth* **by William Shakespeare**
Question 1 (b), 2009 exam

1. (b) Did you feel sympathy for Lady Macbeth at any time during the play? Give reasons for your answer, based on your knowledge of the text. (10 marks)

#### SAMPLE ANSWER: 1 (b)

I never liked Lady Macbeth and I still don't like her having studied the play at length. What was she talking about when she said 'unsex me here', did she really want to be a man or what? Plus, a woman that would like to poison her babies with her own milk is a fairly sick individual. She went on to kill herself at the end of the play and while I know suicide is generally frowned on and is a terrible thing, I didn't feel much sympathy for her. Even her husband wasn't too bothered because he said 'she should have died hereafter' i.e. she could have waited till tomorrow. In the version we saw, she came across as completely two-faced by welcoming in the king while just before that she had asked her husband to 'stick his courage to the sticking place' which was really asking him to kill the king. She seemed to go mad for no real reason near the end and this only made me dislike her more.

(175 words approx.)

#### EXAMINER'S ASSESSMENT

- The candidate addresses the question asked but there is an issue with the overall tone and 'register' of this answer. It is quite informal and conversational, despite the essential thrust of the response being broadly correct.

- The candidate has a general grasp of the play but has not looked in much depth at the character of Lady Macbeth.
- Vocabulary is casual and also limited. An average-to-moderate answer overall.
- Marks: 3 (P and C) + 2 (L and M) = 5/10 (D1 grade).

## Below is a 10-mark question about setting.

*The Great Gatsby* **by F. Scott Fitzgerald**

1. (a) Describe Gatsby's house as we see it at the very end of the novel. Refer to the text in your answer. (10 marks)

### SAMPLE ANSWER: 1 (a)

Gatsby's mansion is a wreck at the end of the story. His world has come to an end and there is nobody to visit him anymore. One car turns up one day without realising that there is nobody there anymore. The grass is grown really long and taxi drivers stop and look into it every so often.

(60 words approx.)

### EXAMINER'S ASSESSMENT

- This answer is too short.
- There is a contradiction in lines 2 and 3.
- There is simply a lack of content here. While the expression is adequate, there is not enough detail in the answer. Perhaps the student did not revise this part of the story well enough.
- Marks: 1 (P and C) + 2 (L and M) = 3/10 (E grade).

> **key point**
> You must be very familiar with all of the major issues in your Single Text.

## Below is a 10-mark question about a theme.

*Translations* **by Brian Friel**

1. (a) In *Translations*, Sarah is unable to speak properly. Why is her inability to speak an important feature of the play? (10 marks)

### SAMPLE ANSWER: 1 (a)

I think this play is a lot to do with identity and who people are. Sarah's efforts to pronounce her name is her attempt to let people know who she is and prove that she is a good person. She is considered 'dumb', as it says in the opening notes in the text. She has been like this all her life. This means that she has always been looked down on and her life has not always been the easiest. The action begins with her trying to say her name with Manus's help. He tells her that 'Nothing will stop them now, nothing in the wide world' when she does manage to do it for him. However, when the two soldiers come and Lancey asks her name, she cannot pronounce it. This is a sad moment because it suggests that when the English came to change the place names in Ireland they did more than that. They also brought the local people down because the language of the area was now foreign. Brian Friel uses the character of Sarah to show how important it is that people from different backgrounds understand each other and how important everybody's native language is.

(200 words approx.)

**EXAMINER'S ASSESSMENT**

- This answer has plenty of content and deals in a straightforward way with the question asked.
- The use of the word 'identity' in the first sentence is to be noted. It hints at one of the major themes in the play.
- Some of the vocabulary is basic but it does communicate the candidate's view adequately. A good effort.
- Marks: 5 (P and C) + 3 (L and M) = 8/10 (B1 grade).

**30-MARK QUESTIONS**

The 30-mark question you choose will give you more scope to be creative or analytical. The 30-mark questions often ask you to write a **letter, talk, speech or newspaper article based on your knowledge of the text**. Keep in mind all that you have already learned about **good, coherent writing** for Paper 1. Many of the same skills are needed here to succeed.

This means that all the preparation you have done for the Comprehension (see Chapter 4 of this book) can also be used here for Single Text 30-mark questions. Just make sure you know your text very well and apply the skills you used for answering Comprehension questions.

These questions ask you to **evaluate** or explain a **personal opinion** on the text. You are giving an opinion on what you have read or seen.

Typical questions include:

- Imagine that you were [character]. How would you…?
- Write a speech in defence of [character].
- Write a magazine article either praising or condemning the text.
- Write a letter to [character] explaining…
- Do you agree with the view that this text is…?
- Which character do you admire most? Why?
- If you were a director, how would you stage…?
- You are asked to play the part of [character]. Explain how you would perform if…

Below is a 30-mark question on *Sive* by John B. Keane
Question C 3 (ii), 2010 exam
3. (ii) Write a piece beginning with one of the following statements:
- I feel sorry for Sive because…
- I feel angry with Mena Glavin because…

(30 marks)

## SAMPLE ANSWER: 3 (ii)

I feel sorry for Sive because the real tragedy of this play is that she is subject to continuous abuse and torment which she does not deserve at all. For starters, Mena uses numerous labels for the orphaned Sive such as 'bye-child' and 'her ladyship' to keep reminding her that her parents are no longer around. Each day she wakes up and goes to school but each day she comes home to a house full of bitterness and resentment. Mena resents the fact that Sive is in school, not because she is against education necessarily but because it is causing them financial hardship. She has had a hard life herself and remembers the hardships she put up with at Sive's age:

> *When I was her age in my father's house, I worked from dawn to dark to put aside my fortune.*

This harsh attitude to life, shaped by the social circumstances in rural Kerry of the 1950s, is a not a place where a vulnerable girl like Sive will be taken care of.

Nanna is an image of an older Ireland, the lady by the fire smoking the pipe and retaining a sense of decency and morality. However, Nanna does nothing to improve Mena's attitudes as she sees her as almost worthless to the family given that she is childless:

> *Every woman of your age in the parish has a child of her own.*

This hangs over the family home like a curse at a time when marriage and children were the bedrock of a stable society. The effect of all this bitterness is that Sive is the one who is at the receiving end of much of the frustration and anger in the household. Mena comes across as quite a formidable character whose bullying nature is the result of years of this type of frustration. Nanna has Sive's best interests at heart but at her age is quite powerless to do much to save her from the planning and scheming of Mena and Thomasheen. Her uncle Mike is rightly described as a 'man of straw' by his wife: he wants to protect Sive but ultimately he is weak and gives in to the scheming of Thomasheen.

I also feel very sorry for Sive because the one ray of hope in her life is her true love, Liam Scuab. Once again, her life path is dictated by others who see Sive a type of 'cash-cow' to get them out of difficulty. In arranging the marriage to the ancient bachelor Sean Dota, to some extent Mena, Thomasheen and Mike all serve to send Sive to her tragic death out on the bog. It is hard to know whether she committed suicide or whether she just fell in a hole. Whatever the case, I have great sympathy for Sive who is very much an innocent victim of other people's bitterness and greed at a time of real hardship in rural Ireland.

(480 words approx.)

## EXAMINER'S ASSESSMENT

- Plenty of detail here for a 30-mark question and the candidate demonstrates a very good grasp of the main issues concerning the characters.
- The answer links sympathy for Sive to the attitudes and behaviour of the other main characters; this avoids excessive summary.
- The level of expression is also very good: the sentences are well phrased and the vocabulary is broad and varied.
- There are a number of appropriate quotations here also.
- Marks: 8 (P) + 8 (C) + 8 (L) + 3 (M) = 27/30 (A1 grade).

**key point**

The writing skills needed for Paper 1 are just as important for Paper 2.

# 7 The Comparative Study

**aims**
- To understand the **modes of comparison**.
- To learn a **method of revision** for this section, understanding the **importance of comparisons as well as contrasts**.

The Comparative Study section accounts for 17.5 per cent of the entire exam. It carries 70 marks, which is more than the Single Text section. This section can include plays, novels, autobiography, films and other types of writing. Your teacher should have covered two (possibly even three) such texts. Many Ordinary Level students may not have studied a Shakespearean play and the exam allows for this.

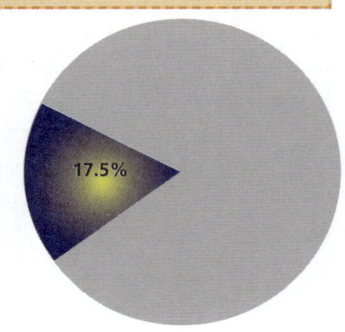

17.5%

It is likely that a film is one of your choices and many students find this to be a very enjoyable part of the course. In simple terms, you are required to compare specific aspects of your chosen texts using **modes of comparison**.

| MODES OF COMPARISON | |
|---|---|
| 1. Theme | (2014 & 2015) |
| 2. Relationships | (2014 & 2015) |
| 3. Social setting | (2014) |
| 4. Hero–Heroine–Villain | (2015) |

## Structure of the comparative study section

Use the **3–2–1 formula** for remembering how the Comparative Study section is structured on your exam paper.

- **Three** modes of comparison are prescribed for each year.
- **Two** will appear on the exam paper.
- **One** question – **parts (a) and (b)** – is all that you must do.

Identify which modes are relevant for your year of examination and **thoroughly revise two modes**. This is sufficient to have you prepared for the exam.

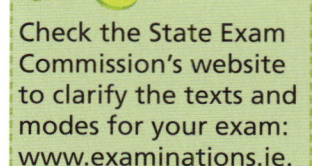

**key point**
Check the State Exam Commission's website to clarify the texts and modes for your exam: www.examinations.ie.

**key point**
Even if you covered three modes in class, revise just **two** of them for the exam.

Some other points to remember when preparing for this section of the exam:
- You cannot just tell the story of your chosen texts. The purpose of this section is to **test your skills of comparison**.
- This means being able to spot aspects of the texts that are similar. It also involves highlighting differences. You are asked to **compare and contrast** and that is what you are marked on.
- The best approach is not to revise all of the material in each text. Instead, focus on a number of **key moments** in each text, which will provide you with the material for exam answers.
- Key moments are often moments of revelation, discovery, choice, tension or climax. Key moments often bring about some kind of change.
- Experience shows that **the same key moments in a text often work with any of the modes**. Be careful in choosing moments or scenes; ensure that they have a major bearing on the story.
- **Be very careful not to confuse the Single Text with the Comparative Texts.** This will lead to automatic disqualification of marks by the examiner.
- At ordinary level, you **do not have to study Shakespeare** for the Comparative Study section.

**key point**
Compare key moments or scenes in your texts. Choose the moments wisely!

# Film

The inclusion of film on the Comparative Study section has proven to be very popular. Films can be studied just like any other text, but it is worth noting these points:
- Films **show** you a story; they don't just tell you something. The **theme** of a film is contained in what you see and hear.
- Look carefully at how **colour** is used for effect.
- Be aware of how **sound** and **music** influence your reaction to the story and characters. This includes the soundtrack and the musical score (background or incidental music).
- Films are always located in a certain place and time, a **social setting** with a particular atmosphere.
- Look at how **actors** behave at key moments. How are relationships shaped and developed?
- Films contain great moments of **tension** and **climax**. Know when these occur and remember the resolution (how it all ends).
- Consider from whose **point of view** we see the action unfold. What are we being shown? What or who can we not see?
- What is the main **theme** of the film? All film-makers have something to tell us, which is shown in the work they create. Know exactly what that point is before continuing to revise for your exam. Start by jotting down the main themes of your studied film.

# Questions asked

**Two modes** will appear on your exam paper. It is likely that you will also have a **choice within the mode**: an A or B option. For example, if you choose to do the **Theme** mode, you will have **two sets of questions** and **you must do one**.

> Always read the exam paper very carefully!

The exam questions are usually split into **two parts**, with the marks divided 30/40:

- The **30-mark question** usually asks about a **mode** of comparison in **one** text.
- The **40-mark question** will require a longer answer. This is where the real business of **comparison with another text (or texts)** takes place.

## 30-mark questions

The 30-mark questions usually appear as part (a) of a two-part question. You will most likely be asked to write about one text. **You should practise doing short essays (200–300 words) on different modes appearing in one text.**

Recent 30-mark exam questions include the following.

- Name a **theme** from one of your comparative texts. Show how this theme plays an important part in the story.
- Describe **one significant relationship** in one of your chosen texts.
- Choose one of your comparative texts and **outline a relationship that had a strong impact** on you.
- Describe the **social setting** of one of your comparative texts and say whether or not it appealed to you.
- Choose a **person** from one of your texts in your comparative course whose **behaviour you admired or did not admire** and write a short account of him or her.

## 40-mark questions

The 40-mark questions usually appear as part (b) of a two-part question. **They require you to compare what you have written in (a) to another text you studied.** You must stick to the question asked and remember your key moments.

Recent 40-mark exam questions include the following.

- Show how the **same theme** was **portrayed differently** in another text from your course.
- Choose a **relationship from another text which was different to the one outlined in (a)**. Say what made this relationship different.
- Choose a **relationship from another text** from your course. Explain **what was different about the impact** this had on you.
- Describe **the social setting of another text** from your comparative studies and show the **similarities and/or differences** that you found when compared to the text in (a). Refer to each text in making your points.

- Choose a **character from another text** from your comparative course. **Compare him or her with the person you have chosen in (a) and say which of the two you preferred.**

## Choosing the right questions

Read the following questions on **Theme** taken from the 2007 paper. Hopefully you will spot something that might help you in choosing questions on the day.

> **exam Q**
>
> **THEME**
>
> 1. (a) Describe how your chosen theme is presented in **one** of the texts.
>
>    (30 marks)
>
>    (b) Compare the way in which the same theme is presented in a **second** text with the way it has been presented in the text in (a) above.
>
>    To begin your answer use one of the following statements:
>    - 'I thought the theme in my first text was more powerful/less powerful than the theme in my second text because …'
>    - 'I enjoyed the theme of one text more than the other because …'
>
>    (40 marks)
>
>    or
>
> 2. (a) Write a piece in which you attempt to persuade a reader that a theme is presented in a more interesting way in **one text rather than in another**.
>    Support your views with reference to the **two texts chosen**.
>
>    (30 marks)
>
>    (b) Select one moment from each of **two** texts that you have studied that appeals to you in a special way. Say how, in your opinion, these moments have helped you to understand the theme involved. Explain your answer with references to your chosen texts.
>
>    (40 marks)

**Did you spot that Question 1 is much easier than Question 2?**

A very confident and well-prepared student might fancy **Question 2**, but it **means that you must compare two texts right from the start and for both parts (a) and (b).**

**Question 1 (a)** asks for a response to **one text only**. **Part (b)** asks to **compare it with one other text** and even gives you the first sentence to get you going!

From time to time, the Comparative Study questions are written like this, so read carefully before you choose your option on the day.

> **exam focus**
>
> Of all the sections in Paper 2, the Comparative Study section requires the most careful reading of the questions.

## Preparing for the exam

The first thing a student must do to revise the Comparative Study is to ask: **which is my favourite text?** Consider the two or three Comparative Texts you have studied (do not include your Single Text) and choose one to use as a base or anchor for your answers.

**For illustration, let's choose an anchor text that is a film.** *I'm Not Scared* **is a film by Gabriele Salvatores.**

**key point**
Your favourite or **anchor** text is the one you can write about most clearly and confidently in the exam.

**exam focus**
Be sure to include the names of your chosen texts and their authors/directors every time you answer an exam question.

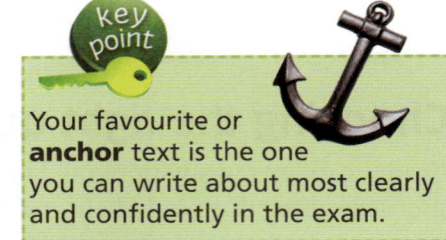

You should make a list of **key moments** or scenes in your text. For *I'm Not Scared* this could be:

- Key moment 1: Opening Credits – rising from the dark to the sunlight.
- Key moment 2: Discovery of Filippo in the hole.
- Key moment 3: Pino returns with gifts for the family.
- Key moment 4: Arrival of the mobile shop – second-hand shopping.
- Key moment 5: Bringing food to Filippo.
- Key moment 6: Argument in the house with Sergio.
- Key moment 7: Removing Filippo from the hole.
- Key moment 8: The tragic conclusion.

**After this analysis of your anchor text, choose a second text. For illustration, we'll examine** *How Many Miles to Babylon?* **by Jennifer Johnston.**

Make a list of **key moments.** For *How Many Miles to Babylon?* this could be:

- Key moment 1: The opening – Alec reflecting.
- Key moment 2: Depiction of the 'unwelcoming' dining room.
- Key moment 3: Alec and Jerry meet and become friends.

**key point**
Once you have examined an anchor text and a second text in this way, you have the **raw material for any question** that can appear on your exam paper.

THE COMPARATIVE STUDY 69

- Key moment 4: Encountering Major Glendinning.
- Key moment 5: Alec arguing with the Major to save Jerry's execution.
- Key moment 6: Alec shoots Jerry and awaits his own execution.

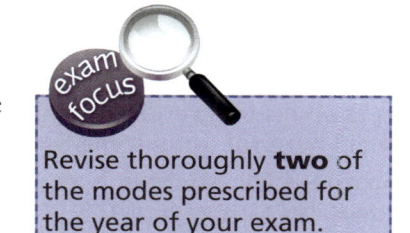

> **exam focus**
> Revise thoroughly **two** of the modes prescribed for the year of your exam.

**exam Q**

Look at the options given in 2008. The **mode** is **relationships**. Can you spot which question is the easier option?

## Relationships

1. (a) 'Relationships can be very complicated.'
    Describe a relationship which you have studied in one of the texts on your comparative course, and explain why you found it to be complicated. (30 marks)
   (b) Choose a relationship from another text on your comparative course and explain why you found this relationship more or less complicated than the one you described in (a). Remember to refer to both relationships in the course of your answer. (40 marks)

    or

2. (a) Briefly describe a relationship from each of **two** of the three texts you have studied on your comparative course. (30 marks)
   (b) Explain why you think one of the relationships you described in (a) is more successful than the other. Remember to refer to both relationships in the course of your answer. (40 marks)

Question 1 appears to be a bit easier than Question 2, so let's look at a sample answer for Question 1. Important phrases have been put in bold.

### SAMPLE ANSWER: 1 (a)

I have studied the film *I'm Not Scared* which is set in southern Italy in the late 1970s. It is directed by Gabriele Salvatores. There is a very **interesting and complicated relationship at the centre of the story and this is what makes the movie most appealing to me.** The backdrop to the movie is the political and social unrest between the wealthy north of the country and the poorer, rural south. Children from wealthy northern families are kidnapped and held for ransom in the south and this is how this film unfolds.

Michele is a ten-year-old boy from the rural village of Acqua Traverse. He spends his days playing with the other village children including his little sister, Maria. One day, he makes a startling discovery: a boy is held prisoner in a hole at an abandoned farmhouse. Through a number of different encounters, **he manages to befriend this boy who we learn**

**is named Filippo.** He is from Milan. We also discover that he is very confused and at one point he shouts 'morto!' meaning that he is 'dead'. The scars on his body and his thin, frail appearance indicate that he has been held here for quite some time.

**The problem for Michele is that he realises the truth of the situation**. His father, Pino, who cares for his wife and children, is involved in a kidnapping conspiracy headed by a man named Sergio. When Michele overhears an argument in his parents' house in which Sergio pulls a gun, Michele fears for Filippo's safety. Rather than free the boy without the money, they threaten to cut off his ears to put more pressure on Filippo's family. Michele by this point feels he must act to free Filippo. However, his newfound friendship with Filippo potentially puts the family relationships in jeopardy, as well as the stability of the whole village, which appears to be in on the kidnapping all along. His mother cares deeply for him and all through we notice how tense and nervous she is. She realises that Michele knows the truth and pleads with him to 'leave this place' when he is old enough. **In the end, the complicated relationship that Michele has with Filippo reaches a tragic end**: in freeing Filippo, Michele is accidently shot by Pino, his own father. This movie shows how **childhood friendships can be ruined by the arrival of the harsh outside world of adulthood** and the death of a young person's innocence.

(420 words approx.)

**EXAMINER'S ASSESSMENT**

- The question is addressed adequately. There is a good summary of the main relationship between the two boys.
- Expression is very good throughout.
- More quotation and references to indicate the closeness between the boys would improve the grade.
- Marks: 8 (P) + 6 (C) + 7 (L) + 3 (M) = 24/30 (B1 grade).

**SAMPLE ANSWER: 1 (b)**

I have also studied the novel *How Many Miles to Babylon?* by Jennifer Johnston. The main relationship in this book is between the two protagonists, Alec Moore and Jerry Crowe, both soldiers in the British Army during World War One. **Unlike the children of the movie *I'm Not Scared*, these two characters have a much more complicated relationship, even though at first, we can see some similarities**.

The two men come from very different social backgrounds, **which is similar to the situation of Michele and Filippo**. Alec is part of the Anglo-Irish aristocracy, lives on an estate in Wicklow with his upper-class parents and enjoys many privileges, **not unlike the wealthy people of Milan**. Jerry comes from working-class stock, eats a basic diet and milks cows with his mother. He must leave school at an early age to provide for the family, **not unlike the situation for Michele in Acqua Traverse**. When they first meet, Alec notices immediately that Jerry appears poorly nourished being 'much smaller than I was, with twig-like bones' and finds his proper name 'Jeremiah' quite unusual, as it is 'not a typical peasant name'.

Their initial friendship is hampered by the fact that they come from the extremes of wealth and poverty in their society and neither set of parents nor the social classes would quickly approve of it. **But in the way that children can be the same around the world, they do manage to form a friendship** mostly because Alec does not share the same regard for social class that his parents and their associates show. Neither is he too concerned with the religious divide that affects them, as he is a Protestant and Jerry a Catholic. However, once Alec's mother Alicia hears of this friendship, she puts a stop to it and says 'No more Jerry' before taking Alec on a trip to Europe. However, both boys hope that one day they will grow up and set up a riding school together. **Like Michele and Filippo, this friendship survives despite all of the pressures on it to end.**

Both young men enlist with the British Army to serve during the war and, not surprisingly, Alec is made an officer and Jerry is sent to the frontline. Their relationship is made even more complicated by the callous Major Glendinning, who commands Alec to execute Jerry (who is accused of being a deserter). It is extremely sad and depressing to see the inhumanity of life in the trenches leading to this type of conclusion. The two young men who had shared a deep friendship and hoped for a future together after the war, now come face to face at the end of a gun. Alec decides to see Jerry in his cell the night before the execution and remarks poignantly that 'what damn fools we were to come, you and I'. This is perhaps an admission of the fact that by going to war, their long-standing friendship was doomed from the start. **While Michele attempts to save Filippo by freeing him, Alec attempts the same with Jerry by shooting him then and there, sparing him the firing squad.** It is an extremely gloomy but powerful act on the part of Alec who pays for his actions by being sentenced to his own execution, as indicated by the opening scene of the novel.

**Unlike the film, which casts Michele as a hero, Alec's loyalty to his friend and his noble action brings about a despairing and gloomy air to the conclusion: he kills the only true friend he had.** While the police arrive in Acqua Traverse and Sergio is likely to face justice, there is no real sense of satisfaction at the end of the novel.

(620 words approx.)

### EXAMINER'S ASSESSMENT

- Good treatment of the question and a good knowledge of the relationship between the two main characters.
- The comparative phrases and points made are adequate and quotation is supplied.
- There could be some more focus on exactly why this was 'more complicated' than the other text.
- All-round, a very good attempt.
- Marks: 11 (P) + 10 (C) + 10 (L) + 4 (M) = 35/40 (A1 grade).

# Useful phrases

There are certain words and phrases that are useful for the Comparative Study. Examiners are on the lookout for them. Provided they are accurate and relevant, you stand a greater chance of scoring well in this section if you include certain phrases. Try to incorporate the following phrases into your answers:

## When looking for similarities:

- 'In both texts…'
- 'Similarly to text A, text B…'
- 'I also noted/found/saw/felt that…'
- 'This also occurs/happens/exists in…'
- 'When we look at text B…'
- 'Text A and B both show/demonstrate/indicate/portray…'
- 'In the same way…'
- 'Once again, we see that…'

## When looking for differences:

- 'In contrast…'
- 'Unlike in text A…'
- 'What a difference from…'
- 'This is the reverse of…'
- 'This is the opposite to…'
- 'I found that text B differs…'
- 'While X happens in text A, Y happens in text B…'

## Essential words and phrases:

- Unlike
- Like
- Similar
- Different
- Contrastingly
- Too
- Also
- Yet
- But
- Whereas
- On the other hand
- However
- Nevertheless
- Consequently
- As a result
- Therefore

# 8 Poetry

**aims**
- To gain an **understanding of poetic technique** and the terminology used by poets.
- To examine the **Unseen Poem** and to learn how it helps with revision generally.
- To become familiar with the **Studied Poetry** and learn a method of revision for it.

The Poetry section accounts for 17.5 per cent of the exam. The Unseen Poem amounts to 5 per cent and the Studied Poetry is 12.5 per cent.

17.5%

## Poetic terms

Let's remind ourselves of some important technical terms in poetry.

- **Alliteration** occurs when the same consonants are used repeatedly at the beginnings of words in close succession. For example: 'the wisest wizard' (Hardy).
- **Assonance** occurs when similar sounding vowels create a particular sound effect. For example: 'fierce tears' (Thomas).
- **Imagery** is hugely important in poetry. Images create pictures in the reader's mind that affect their feelings or reaction to the poem's subject matter. Images can be seen (visual), heard (aural) or felt (tactile). All poetry contains some imagery. For example: 'a dirty dog, quite comfy' (Bishop).
- **Language**: Poems are a shortened or compressed form of communication. The language of poetry is highly charged and it is used in creative ways.

Robert Frost

Seamus Heaney

Dylan Thomas

Sylvia Plath

Language techniques like assonance, simile, metaphor, etc. recur in poetry.
- **Metaphor** is when a word or phrase is used to describe something in a non-literal way. Much poetry is metaphoric: it aims to describe things in colourful, abstract ways. For example: 'The Cage' (Montague) can be understood as an entirely metaphoric description of how the speaker's father lived.
- **Onomatopoeia** occurs when the sound of a word reflects its meaning. For example: 'unintelligible syllables' in Sylvia Plath's 'The Arrival of the Bee Box' captures this perfectly.
- **Personification** is when human characteristics are given to inanimate objects. Metaphorically, life is given to lifeless things. For example: 'In the sun the slagheap slept' appears in "The Explosion" by Philip Larkin.
- **Pun**: A pun is a play on words that creates a double meaning. Sometimes the effect is comic; sometimes not. For example: 'The boy saw all' in Robert Frost's 'Out, Out—' is terrifying in its impact.
- **Simile**: This is a description that uses 'as' or 'like' to make a comparison between two related subjects. It is related to metaphor in that the things being compared may not have an obvious likeness. For example: 'Like dolmens round my childhood' (Montague).
- **Speaker**: This is the voice in a poem. It is incorrect to assume that the poet is the voice in a poem, although they often are. For example: 'Daniel's Duck' by Kerry Hardie begins with 'I'. But is it the poet or somebody else speaking?
- **Stanza**: This is the correct term for lines that are grouped together in a poem. It is sometimes confused with verse, which originally applied to music rather than poetry.
- **Theme**: This is the main idea in a poem. It is not necessarily the subject matter, but rather the deeper concern that is raised or discussed in the poem. For example: Yeats considers the theme of 'balance' both in life itself and on-board a plane in his poem 'An Irish Airman Foresees His Death'.
- **Tone** is associated with feeling or mood. One can imagine the tone of the poem being the sound of the voice that speaks in the poem. It creates the atmosphere or mood of the situation. There is a strong tone of anxiety in the young speaker's voice in Heaney's 'A Constable Calls'.

Of this list, the most important terms to focus on in exam answers are: **theme**, **imagery**, **language** and **tone** (**TILT**).

## How to study poetry for the Leaving Certificate

How should you study poetry for the Leaving Certificate? Should you learn each poem off by heart, like generations of students that have come before? You

> **key point**
> Those who understand are likely to remember; those who just memorise don't always understand.

could do this, but nowadays many people believe that **understanding** is more important than **memorising**.

In getting to the heart of what a poem is about, we are trying to understand the issues or concerns of the poet. This means understanding the **theme** of the poem. In doing this, a student must first ask: *how do I learn?* This is particularly relevant regarding poetry, since it is a very different type of writing. Words are rarely taken literally in poetry and this presents us with a challenge. What should we do?

## The see–hear–feel approach

Each of us can *look* at poetry, *listen* to poetry and *be affected* by poetry. However, some scientists believe that each one of us is instinctively drawn towards one of these sensory reactions more than the other two. So while we may all have eyes, ears and feelings, each of us reacts in an individual way when learning, even though we might not be aware of this.

This means that students are either:

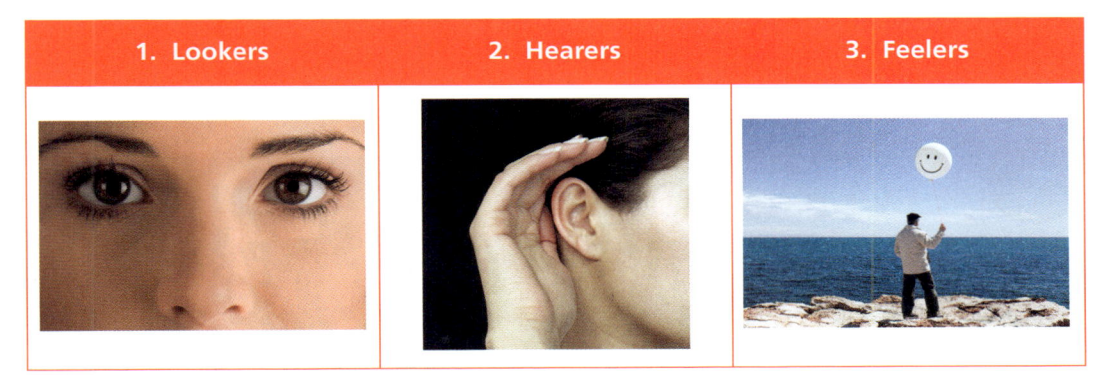

| 1. Lookers | 2. Hearers | 3. Feelers |
|---|---|---|

So how does this relate to the Leaving Certificate exam?

Start with the **Unseen Poem**. Choose a poem from any exam paper and ignore the questions for now. Just read the poem slowly with a pen and paper in hand. Then break everything down into three categories:

> **key point**
> Discover whether you are mostly a looker, hearer or feeler. This will really help you understand **how** you learn things.

1. What do you **see** when you read the poem for the first time? Jot down a quick list of **images** that come to mind on reading the poem. This will give you a sense of place, setting and time. Can you imagine people or creatures involved in some activity? The images in a poem can be extremely varied.

2. **Recite** the poem in your head or aloud if you can. Try to **hear** what the poet is saying. You may get a sense of rhyme in the poem. Or you may respond to the beat or rhythm (metre). Alliteration, assonance and other sound effects may also be prominent.

3. Now read the poem and try to identify the main **feeling** or tone. Is there **bitterness, disappointment, regret, fear, excitement, joy** or **mystery** in the voice of the speaker?

There may be more than one feeling communicated but the Ordinary Level poems usually have **one strong emotion** that the poet intends to communicate.

What did this process do for your understanding of the poem? Were you a:

| 1. Looker | 2. Hearer | 3. Feeler |
|---|---|---|
| You could really see the **imagery** in the poem. You saw colours, shapes and faces of people. You had a clear picture of the location or setting. | You could really hear the beat and rhythm of the poem. You appreciated the way **language** was used. The words sounded well to you and you liked any rhyming or musical qualities in the poem. | You were affected emotionally by the poem. You could sense the different **tones**. The poem made an impact on you and you could relate to the experience of the speaker. You had **strong feelings** on reading the poem. |

It is likely that you had a stronger sense of one of these elements: seeing, hearing or feeling. Maybe you had aspects of each. When you put all three elements together, you are well on your way to understanding the meaning of the poem and its **themes** should become clearer to you.

**key point**

Understanding poetry means identifying the **theme** (the main issue or idea) and considering the **imagery, language and tone**.

**exam Q**

Below is an Unseen Poetry question from the 2005 exam paper.

## Unseen Poem: 20 marks

Read this poem at least twice and then respond to the questions that follow.

The Scottish poet, Douglas Dunn, writes a poem in which he explores his feelings about a family leaving their home in the city.

### A REMOVAL FROM TERRY STREET

On a squeaking cart, they push the usual stuff,
A mattress, bed ends, cups, carpets, chairs,
Four paperback westerns. Two whistling youths
In surplus US Army battle-jackets
Remove their sister's goods. Her husband
Follows, carrying on his shoulders the son
Whose mischief we are glad to see removed,
And pushing, of all things, a lawnmower.
There is no grass in Terry Street. The worms
Come up cracks in concrete yards in moonlight.
That man, I wish him well. I wish him grass.

1. What kind of world is being described in this poem? Refer to the poem in your answer. **(10 marks)**
2. How, in your opinion, does the writer feel about the family that is leaving Terry Street? Refer to the text of the poem in your answer. **(10 marks)**

Before we examine a sample answer to these questions, consider what you've learned about the See–Hear–Feel approach. Note that Question 1 asks you to **describe what you see and hear** in the world of the poem. Question 2 is all about **feeling**: what does the poet feel when his family leave Terry Street?

As always, remember the golden rule of **answering the question that is asked**. Also, you should follow the **statement–quotation–comment** format in all of your answers.

### SAMPLE ANSWER: 1

The world of this poem is an urban one, where poverty is apparent. The fact that 'there is no grass on Terry Street' tells me that this must be in a town or city and the poet seems to be laughing at the fact that the family have a lawnmower. The brothers are wearing 'surplus US Army battle-jackets' and are pushing a cart with all the family belongings. They are not moving house but instead are being 'removed' as the title says. I think that this may be because they cannot afford the rent or are being re-housed because of anti-social behaviour, maybe caused by the son who sits on the father's shoulders.

(110 words approx.)

### EXAMINER'S ASSESSMENT

- This is a really good answer for a ten-mark question. It makes an excellent opening claim that is well supported with five pieces of evidence.
- The reference to the title is apt and it shows that the candidate has read the poem closely.
- Marks: 6 (P and C) + 4 (L and M) = 10/10 (A1 grade).

### SAMPLE ANSWER: 2

I think that the poet has some sympathy for the family. It is contained mostly in the final line. When he says 'I wish him well', I feel that he understands the shame and hardship that comes if you are thrown out of your house. He sees that the man is doing his best for his family, having a lawnmower that might be used if they get a better house or could make some money if he sells it. He is glad that the son is going ('whose mischief we are glad to see going'), but overall he does feel a bit sorry for them.

(110 words approx.)

### EXAMINER'S ASSESSMENT

- This is a really good answer that includes the key word 'sympathy' in the opening sentence.
- Two quotations are included to back up the claim and the candidate addresses the question competently.
- Marks: 6 (P and C) + 4 (L and M) = 10/10 (A1 grade).

**Key point:** Students who can **identify feelings** in a poem typically score well in their answers.

# Unseen poem

The Unseen Poem is not too complicated. You will be asked for a reaction to specific issues after some careful reading. The purpose of this section of the exam is to **test your response to poetry generally** before tackling specific prescribed poetry.

- Following the Unseen Poem there are usually **two short questions worth 10 marks each**.
- Answers of about **100 words** are usually sufficient.
- Remember to stick to the **statement–quotation–comment** formula.
- Occasionally the paper has one long 20-mark question. **Keep an eye out for the marks allotted on your exam paper.** If you see a 20-mark question after the Unseen Poem, simply follow the answering process as normal, but write twice as much as you would for a ten-mark question.

**Questions on the Unseen Poem often relate to:**

- **Feelings** expressed in the poem.
- **Imagery** in the poem and how it sets the scene.
- **Sound effects** and the use of language.
- **Themes**, i.e. what is the main idea?
- Your **reaction** to the poem. Did you like it or not like it? Why?

> **key point**
> As part of your revision you should spend time looking at Unseen Poems in past exam papers. Doing this will make you more familiar with poetic technique and terminology.

---

**exam Q**

Below is an Unseen Poetry question from the 2008 exam paper.

## Unseen Poem: 20 marks

Read the following poem and the two questions on it at least twice before writing your answers.

**SEAGULL**

We are the dawn marauders.*
We prey on pizza. We kill kebabs.
We mug thrushes for bread crusts
with a snap of our big bent beaks.
We drum the worms from the ground
with the stamp of our wide webbed feet.
We spread out, cover the area –
like cops looking for the body
of a murdered fish-supper.
Here we go with our hooligan yells
loud with gluttony, sharp with starvation.
Here we go bungee-jumping on the wind,

charging from the cold sea of our birth.
This is invasion. This is occupation.
Our flags are black, white and grey.
Our wing-stripes are our rank.
No sun can match the brazen
colour of our mad yellow eyes.

We are the seagulls.
We are the people.
**Brian McCabe**

*(raiders/robbers)

1. In this poem the poet vividly describes the actions and conduct of seagulls. Choose **two** of these descriptions which appeal to you most. Explain your choices. (10 marks)
2. *We are the seagulls.*
   *We are the people.*
   From your reading of the poem, what similarities do you think the poet draws between seagulls and humans? Explain your answer. (10 marks)

## SAMPLE ANSWER: 1

I like when he says that the seagulls are like cops looking for a body and when they have mad yellow eyes. The cops are the police so I think he means that the seagulls are like them. People don't like the cops and sometimes seagulls are not liked either. Maybe it's just that they have to do a job when they need to find food they have to kill other animals. Their eyes are mad and yellow and this makes them seem like fierce and wicked birds. Overall, it is a really vivid description.

(100 words approx.)

## EXAMINER'S ASSESSMENT

- The candidate engages with the task and does answer the question asked. Two examples are selected, although there is little elaboration on them.
- The candidate tries to give a personal interpretation of the scene. Therefore, in spite of poor language skills and expression, this merits at least a pass mark.
- Marks: 3 (P and C) + 2 (L and M) = 5/10 (D1 grade).

## SAMPLE ANSWER: 2

The seagulls are very like humans the way they kill things and cause trouble for others. 'Here we go with our hooligan yells' is like the way mad football fans riot and cause fights all over the place. I didn't think hooligans were like birds, they are more like wild animals when they get going. I seen many hooligans on the telly but none of them looked like seagulls. But then again, the birds here are described like people so maybe next time I see a seagull, I will think of them as vicious birds that cause trouble for other creatures around them, just like hooligans do.

(110 words approx.)

### EXAMINER'S ASSESSMENT

- This is an excellent example of a candidate with limited skills really trying to say as much as they can to earn marks.
- Crucially, the basic question is answered: birds are equated with hooligans. The candidate expands on that idea with reference to the poem and some personal input.
- Marks: 5 (P and C) + 2 (L and M) = 7/10 (B3 grade).

Overall grade for Unseen Poetry section is 12/20: C2.

These sample answers scored a C2 grade overall, in spite of what the examiner described as 'limited' writing skills. While the student did not have a sophisticated style of writing, they answered the questions in their own way. They used the statement–quotation–comment formula and, crucially, they gave the impression that they really wanted to do their best.

## Studied poetry

**Four poems** from your full list will appear on the exam paper. Each year, the exam papers have shown that **two poems come from a list studied by both Higher and Ordinary Level students**. The other **two poems come from a list confined to Ordinary Level students only.**

You need to familiarise yourself with the two lists of poems: List A and List B. This is very important in terms of revision if you have been in a class with mixed Higher and Ordinary Level students. It is important that you revise **one list only**. The list you choose to work on will depend on what material you covered in the two years of your Leaving Certificate cycle.

Examine the lists opposite very carefully.

> **key point**
> You are not asked to 'explain away' the Unseen Poem. Rather, the focus is on what the poem says to you. **Always remember to answer the questions asked**.

> **key point**
> It is not necessary to revise all 36 poems for your exam. Depending on your teacher's approach, **choose one list or the other** for revision!

## 2014 exam

### List A: Higher & Ordinary Levels

|  |  |
|---|---|
| Boland: | The Fish / The Prodigal / Filling Station |
| Dickinson: | I felt a Funeral / I heard a fly buzz |
| Heaney: | A Constable Calls / The Underground / A Call |
| Kinsella: | Thinking of Mr D / Mirror in February |
| Larkin: | Ambulances / The Explosion |
| Mahon: | Grandfather / After the Titanic / Antarctica |
| Plath: | Poppies in July / Child / The Arrival of the Bee Box |
| Yeats: | The Wild Swans at Coole / An Irish Airman Foresees His Death |

**20 poems**

### List B: Ordinary Level only

|  |  |
|---|---|
| Beer: | The Voice |
| Duffy: | Valentine |
| Gallagher: | The Hug |
| Hardie: | Daniel's Duck |
| Herbert: | The Collar |
| Kennelly: | Night Drive |
| Lochhead: | Kidspoem/Bairnsang |
| Nemerov: | Wolves in the Zoo |
| O'Callaghan: | The Net |
| Piercy: | Will We Work Together? |
| Shuttle: | Zoo Morning |
| Sirr: | Madly Singing in the City |
| Thomas: | Do not go gentle into that good night |
| Wheatley: | Chronicle |
| Williams: | This is just to say… |
| Wyley: | Poems for Breakfast |

**16 poems**

## 2015 exam

### List A: Higher & Ordinary Levels

|  |  |
|---|---|
| Dickinson: | I felt a Funeral / I heard a fly buzz |
| Donne: | The Flea / Song: Go and Catch a Falling Star |
| Frost: | The Tuft of Flowers / Mending Wall / 'Out, out—' |
| Hardy: | The Darkling Thrush / During Wind and Rain |
| Montague: | The Cage / The Locket / Like Dolmens Round My Childhood |
| Ní Chuilleanáin: | Street / The Bend in the Road / 'To Niall Woods…' |
| Plath: | Poppies in July / Child / The Arrival of the Bee Box |
| Yeats: | The Wild Swans at Coole / An Irish Airman Foresees his Death |

**20 poems**

### List B: Ordinary Level only

|  |  |
|---|---|
| Auden: | Funeral Blues |
| Bryce: | Self-Portrait in the Dark |
| Delanty: | After Viewing *The Bowling Match at Castlemary, Cloyne* (1847) |
| Duffy: | Valentine |
| Hardie: | Daniel's Duck |
| Herbert: | The Collar |
| Hughes: | The Stag |
| Kennelly: | A Glimpse of Starlings |
| Levertov: | An Arrival (north Wales, 1897) |
| Lochhead: | Revelation |
| Morgan: | Strawberries |
| Muldoon: | Anseo |
| Murphy: | Moonshine |
| O'Callaghan: | The Net |
| Shuttle: | Jungian Cows |
| Wall: | Ghost Estate |

**16 poems**

## Questions on Studied Poetry

**Question 1** is usually divided into parts a, b and c. Each part is worth 10 marks. You are usually asked about specific elements in the poem as well as your broader reaction to it.

**Question 1 on the Studied Poems often includes:**

- Specific issues: **content**, **tone**, **imagery**, etc.
- **How** does the poet create an **image**, **atmosphere** or **setting**?
- What do we **learn** from this poem?
- What is your **favourite phrase** or **line** in the poem?
- Why do you think this poem is so **popular**?
- What **questions are raised** by this poem?
- How would you **feel** if you were…?
- What is the **message** of the poem?
- Describe the **relationship** between…

**Question 2** is worth 20 marks and it is a little different. You may be asked to state **what you liked or disliked about the entire poem**. You may be required to use the **poem as an inspiration** for some creative writing. For example, you could be asked:

- To write a letter to the poet.
- To write the diary entries of one of the characters.
- To describe a film based on the poem.
- Would you like to be in this place or situation?
- What would appeal to you or annoy you most about this poem?
- Continue the story outlined in the poem.

> **key point**
> Poetry is all about **engaging** with language and the feelings generated by the poet. Try to understand it and have an opinion.

In recent years, students have had three options on Question 2, so it is really important to read all options carefully and make a sound decision.

## A method for revising Studied Poetry

Below are four prescribed poems. Two are from the combined Higher and Ordinary list; two are from the Ordinary Level only list. The **See–Hear–Feel** method has been applied to each poem to make revision easier. Use this approach to revise a selection of your own chosen poems.

# POETRY

| 'Mirror in February' by Kinsella: 2014, List A ||| 
| --- | --- | --- |
| **See** | **Hear** | **Feel** |
| **Imagery:** misty morning; cold bedroom; man shaving, looking into mirror; growing old; sees trees outside, sees them growing old too; folds towel and leaves. | **Language:** shaven jaw; dry down-turning mouth; crumbling; mirror of my soul; hacked clean for better bearing; brute necessities; grace; not young, not renewable, but man. | **Tone:** tiredness; exhaustion; depression; resignation; acceptance. |

| 'Do Not Go Gentle into That Good Night' by Thomas: 2014, List B |||
| --- | --- | --- |
| **See** | **Hear** | **Feel** |
| **Imagery:** person dying in bed; old man; screaming; trying to beat death; wise men; good men; serious men; sky is blazing with light; speaker's father crying in bed; people praying. | **Language:** good night (pun); burn and rave; rage, rage; dark is right; lightning; dying of the light; blaze like meteors; curse; bless; fierce tears; rage. | **Tone:** desperation; adoration; tension; pleading; hope? |

| 'Child' by Plath: 2015, List A |||
| --- | --- | --- |
| **See** | **Hear** | **Feel** |
| **Imagery:** newborn baby; beautiful blue eyes; animals; zoo; flowers; pools; nervous mother; darkness; fear. | **Language:** absolutely beautiful thing; zoo of the new; stalk without wrinkle; troublous; wringing of hands; dark ceiling without a star; metaphors. | **Tone:** joy; excitement; pure love; despair; depression; terror. |

| 'Funeral Blues' by Auden: 2015, List B |||
| --- | --- | --- |
| **See** | **Hear** | **Feel** |
| **Imagery:** clocks; phone; dog; coffin; funeral procession; aeroplanes; doves; policemen; lovers; stars; night time; gloom; despair. | **Language:** stop all the clocks; dog and bone; moaning overhead; he is Dead; crepe bows; public doves; I was wrong; stars are not wanted now; dismantle the sun. | **Tone:** tiredness; changes to despair and anguish; great pride and love in stanza 3; hopelessness; worrying end – suicidal thoughts? |

After analysing the examples above, you should do the same for the poems you have on your course. Try to **see**, **hear** and **feel** each poem. Then simply answer the questions that follow. It is quite likely that they will be much easier to understand.

## THE WILD SWANS AT COOLE

The trees are in their autumn beauty,
The woodland paths are dry,
Under the October twilight the water
Mirrors a still sky;
Upon the brimming water among the stones
Are nine-and-fifty swans.

The nineteenth autumn has come upon me
Since I first made my count;
I saw, before I had well finished,
All suddenly mount
And scatter wheeling in great broken rings
Upon their clamorous wings.

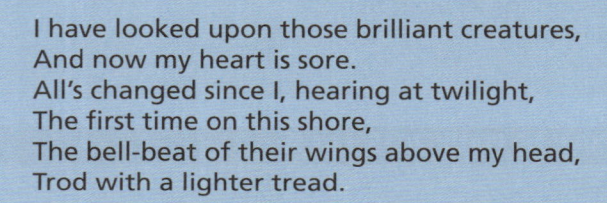

I have looked upon those brilliant creatures,
And now my heart is sore.
All's changed since I, hearing at twilight,
The first time on this shore,
The bell-beat of their wings above my head,
Trod with a lighter tread.

Unwearied still, lover by lover,
They paddle in the cold
Companionable streams or climb the air;
Their hearts have not grown old;
Passion or conquest, wander where they will,
Attend upon them still.

But now they drift on the still water,
Mysterious, beautiful;
Among what rushes will they build,
By what lake's edge or pool
Delight men's eyes when I awake some day
To find they have flown away?

**W. B. Yeats**

1. (a) According to Yeats, what qualities do the swans at Coole Park possess? Explain your answer. (10 marks)
   (b) Which is your favourite stanza in this poem? Explain why you like it. (10 marks)
   (c) This poem presents many pictures (images) to the reader. Choose two which appeal to you and explain why you find them appealing.
   [You may not choose images from the same stanza that you wrote about in 1(b) above.] (10 marks)

2. Answer ONE of the following. Each part carries 20 marks.
   (i) Based on this poem write an article for a travel magazine in which you encourage tourists to visit Coole Park.
   
   or
   
   (ii) *I have looked upon those brilliant creatures,*
   *And now my heart is sore.*
   From your reading of the poem explain why the poet feels like this.
   
   or
   
   (iii) There is another poem by W.B. Yeats on your course, *An Irish Airman Foresees his Death.* Which of these two poems appeals to you more? Give reasons for your answer.

## SAMPLE ANSWER: 1 (a)

The swans are described as mysterious and beautiful. It is interesting to see that they are not described very well until the last stanza. All throughout the poem, the poet lets us imagine what they might be like and then uses these words at the end. It sounds like he has been here before, when he says 'the nineteenth autumn has come upon me/since I first made my count'. The poet has seen the swans many times and now still finds them as mysterious as they were when he first saw them. He also uses the word 'brilliant' to describe them. This is an excellent word to describe their white colour and he is amazed that even though they are older, their hearts remain the same, 'unwearied' by the passage of time. Maybe the poet is envious of these great creatures that seem to live in great peace and harmony after all these years. Yeats is often concerned with love, ageing and the approach of death, so this image of the swans makes him reflect upon his life and how he is feeling. They are also mysterious because he cannot see what is beneath the water or know what is going through their minds at this time.

(200 words approx.)

## EXAMINER'S ASSESSMENT

- This is an excellent response and the question is addressed immediately in the first sentence with the key words 'mysterious' and 'beautiful'.
- Appropriate use of quotation throughout; lots of detail for a 10-mark question.
- There is clarity in what this candidate is saying: the sentence structure and vocabulary are of a very good standard.
- Marks: 6 (P and C) + 4 (L and M) = 10/10 (A1 grade).

## SAMPLE ANSWER: 1 (b)

I really like the fourth stanza. There is personification here because the swans are portrayed as lovers who spend all their time together, both in and out of the water. The words 'lover by lover' create a great image of the swans swimming two-by-two on the lake. This happens in real life: swans mate for life. Maybe the speaker wishes he could be as the swans are, together with a partner for life. I think it is a wonderful image to have in your mind. Yeats creates a very romantic picture here, although it contrasts with the words 'cold' and 'old'. Maybe this is how he feels himself, since Maud Gonne refused his marriage proposals on more than one occasion. Overall, this stanza is very appealing.

(120 words approx.)

### EXAMINER'S ASSESSMENT

- A very good answer, making the connection between the plight of the speaker and the predicament of the swans.
- Appropriate quotation is used and the contrast mentioned near the end is interesting.
- The word 'life' is repeated, but the vocabulary and expression are generally of a very good standard.
- Marks: 6 (P and C) + 3 (L and M) = 9/10 (A1 grade).

### SAMPLE ANSWER: 1 (c)

The first image I like is when the poet says 'now my heart is sore'. He is in some sort of pain, prompted by the picture of the happy swans, swimming together in pairs. There are fifty-nine so this suggests that maybe one swan is lonely and the poet has a connection to that swan. Yeats more than likely is remembering the time when Maud Gonne rejected his proposal, so the image of his heart being sore is very appropriate at this time. I also like the image of the swans that 'have flown away' right at the end. It reminds me of when something close to you dies or passes on and in this case the swans move to their winter home. It is an image of how things always change and how nothing in nature is always the same. This is the theme in this poem, which is that everything changes in nature, even if our love for others is eternal.

(160 words approx.)

### EXAMINER'S ASSESSMENT

- The candidate has provided two images from the relevant stanzas and has addressed the question in a precise way.
- There is an excellent flow to the answer – each sentence builds on the next and the expression is straightforward and well phrased.
- The candidate makes a link between the chosen image and the main concerns of the poem, which is noteworthy.
- Although it is brief, this is an excellent answer.
- Marks: 6 (P and C) + 4 (L and M) = 10/10 (A1 grade).

### SAMPLE ANSWER: 2

Since Question 2 parts (i) and (ii) have already been covered to some extent in other parts of this book, we will tackle part (iii) which has a comparative element to it. This would suit a student who really preferred the other Yeats poetry on the course and would feel comfortable writing about it.

## SAMPLE ANSWER: 2 (iii)

I liked both of the Yeats poems on the course. If I was to choose one it would be 'An Irish Airman Foresees His Death'. I have two reasons.

First, the airman comes across as a much happier speaker than the man at Coole Park. Even though he is way above the clouds and on a mission to drop bombs on the enemy, the airman is still calm and balanced, just like the plane he flies. He is ready to do his duty but he does not hate those he kills, nor love those he is supposed to be 'guarding'. Instead, he is there because he is drawn to the excitement and bravery required to do this job. He is also pretty sure that he will die ('I know that I shall meet my fate') and this does not stop him from carrying out his mission. I admire the airman because he can see a world beyond the war and a life beyond death. Even though war is a terrible thing and people must die, he can detach himself from the politics of it all and just be with himself, above it all, doing his duty as a soldier. The speaker looking at the swans admires their beauty. However, he seems depressed and lonely. Perhaps if he had more energy and a sense of adventure like the airman he wouldn't sound so miserable and unhappy. Maybe his life would feel more worthwhile.

My second reason is that in both poems, Yeats uses a rhyming scheme. However, in 'An Irish Airman Foresees His Death' there is a great rhythm or beat as well. Each line has eight syllables and the way the words sound reminds me of a plane floating and balancing in the air. The final line is a great example of this: 'In balance with this life, this death' creates an image of a small, fragile plane wobbling and balancing through the 'tumult' of the clouds above. I really like this. These are my two reasons for preferring this poem, even though both are very good.

(350 words approx.)

## EXAMINER'S ASSESSMENT

- The candidate shows a very good grasp of the preferred poem. Given that it is not the one on the page, this is to be commended.
- The candidate chooses two specific reasons for the preference and provides quotation to back up their view.
- There is clarity in the answer, which is admirable.
- The candidate takes a dim view of the speaker in the other poem: taking this personal view and providing some back-up with quotation is indicative of a student who has engaged well with the task.
- Overall, a very good response.
- Marks: 12 (P and C) + 8 (L and M) = 20/20 (A1 grade).

Overall grade for Studied Poetry section is 49/50: A1.

# Additional poetic terms

In addition to the poetic terms listed at the start of this chapter, there are some more complicated elements that you should be aware of. Examine the list below very carefully.

**Colloquial language** means everyday speech, some of which can be close to slang. It involves colourful words or phrases understood locally but not universally. For example: 'as cute as they come' (Mahon).

**Elegy**: This is a poem of serious, mournful tone, written because of the death of somebody. Often it is written for a person close to the poet. For example: 'Funeral Blues' by W. H. Auden.

**Hyperbole** is pronounced 'high-per-boh-lay' and is a technical word for exaggeration. Sometimes this extravagant overstatement is used for comedy or ridicule, sometimes just for simple emphasis such as when Kinsella says that 'Mr. D' 'took an hour to drink his glass.'

**Lyric**: A broad term for a personal poem that gives voice to a poet's state of mind or opinion on a topic. Nowadays we associate the word 'lyric' with music (the words of a song).

**Metre** is a French word meaning 'beat' or 'rhythm'. It applies to the emphasis we give to pronouncing certain words in each line or stanza. Some poetic forms, such as blank verse, may have irregular metre. Other forms such as limericks have closely defined metrical rules. Read 'Phenomenal Woman' (Angelou) or 'Antarctica' (Mahon) for good examples of rhythmic poetry.

**Rhetorical question**: This occurs when a question is raised but the answer is: already known; strongly suggested by the questioner; or should be obvious to the reader. For example: 'Why, oh why, the doily?' (Bishop).

**Sarcasm**: A tone of voice that attempts to ridicule or scorn a subject or person. Sometimes referred to as 'the lowest form of wit', effective sarcasm actually requires clever use of language. For example: 'Be careful with that match!' (Bishop).

**Symbol**: This is when an object is used to represent a major idea or principle. Some of the most obvious symbols in poetry are: sunsets (endings or deaths); springtime (new beginnings or births); and colours such as yellow (happiness) and red (anger/desire/danger). Good symbols are understood by a broad audience. Sometimes poets employ unusual symbols to make a point. For example, the 'bell' in Dickinson's 'I felt a Funeral in my Brain' is clearly a symbol of the onset of death and of a church service.

**Syntax** is word order. Poets place words in a certain order in a line to create a desired effect. For example: 'Something there is that doesn't love a wall' in Robert Frost's 'Mending Wall' really emphasises the word 'something' at the very start. This creates a sense of mystery and tension.

**Wit**: A broad term to describe humour or an elevated level of intelligence when applied to writing and language. 'Witty' can mean 'humorous', but wit generally applies to the intellect cleverly at work. For example: Liz Lochead's 'Kidspoem/Bairnsang' is a witty reflection on the differences in accents and understandings of language.

# Final Preparations for Exam Day

## 9 Time-keeping and Revision Checklist

**aims**
- To learn an efficient **time schedule** for the exam papers.
- To develop an effective **checklist for revision**.

## Time schedule for the exam

Students frequently wonder how much they should write in the exam. Rather than thinking in terms of lines or pages, a better question is: **how much can I write in the time allowed?** If the Comprehension B question should take 35 minutes, consider how much you can plan and write in that time. The only real way to find out is to practise answers yourself. Follow the suggested outline below. It takes you through both papers chronologically to show you how your time should be divided.

**exam focus:** These times are approximate. The goal is to answer the questions as best you can in the time allowed.

### Paper 1: Wednesday morning

**9.30a.m.** Begin by reading the entire paper – slowly. Take 10 minutes to read and choose your questions.

**9.40a.m.** Comprehension A (1, 2, 3) carries 50 marks. Allow 35 minutes.

**10.15a.m.** Begin Comprehension B. It carries 50 marks, so allow 35 minutes. Take 5 minutes to plan your piece and 30 minutes to write it.

**10.50a.m.** Begin your Composition plan. Think broadly and try to get your opening and conclusion sorted first. Take 10 minutes to plan your composition.

# TIME-KEEPING AND REVISION CHECKLIST

**11.00a.m.** Start the Composition. It carries 100 marks. You now have 80 minutes to finish the exam. You should use 10 of these 80 minutes to go back over your work. Do not leave early unless you are totally satisfied with your efforts.

**12.20p.m.** Paper 1 ends.

**After Paper 1 you should rest, rest, rest!**

## Paper 2: Thursday afternoon

The Leaving Certificate English timetable was rescheduled a few years back to allow more time between papers. The second paper is now on Thursday afternoon.

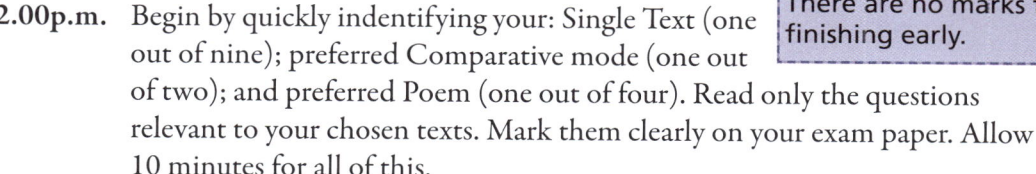

**2.00p.m.** Begin by quickly indentifying your: Single Text (one out of nine); preferred Comparative mode (one out of two); and preferred Poem (one out of four). Read only the questions relevant to your chosen texts. Mark them clearly on your exam paper. Allow 10 minutes for all of this.

**2.10p.m.** Single Text Question 1 (a, b and c). There are 30 marks here, so allow 30 minutes.

**2.40p.m.** Single Text Question 2. There are 30 marks here, so allow 25 minutes. Make a short plan to help you answer this question.

**3.05p.m.** Comparative Study. There are two questions: one with 30 marks and another with 40 marks. Aim to write more on the second question. Allow 65 minutes in total.

**4.10p.m.** Unseen Poetry. Read the poem slowly at least three times. Pause. Answer the two ten-mark questions. Write quickly here. You have only 20 minutes.

**4.30p.m.** Prescribed Poetry. Read your chosen poem twice. You now have 50 minutes to finish the exam. Answer the Prescribed Poetry questions in 40 minutes and leave yourself 10 minutes at the end to look back at your answers.

**5.20p.m.** English Leaving Certificate exam ends.

> **exam focus**
> The exam is not a sprint! There are no marks for finishing early.

> **exam focus**
> Time always flies in exam situations, so don't dwell too much on your work. Check over everything once at the end of the exam.

# Revision checklist

Refer to the checklists below in preparation for your exam. Relevant chapters are listed as a reminder.

## Paper 1 Checklist

- Different **Language Genres**: See Chapters 2, 3, 4 and 5.
  - Informative language
  - Narrative language
  - Persuasive language
  - Argumentative language
  - Aesthetic language
- Two basic writing **styles** (and their variations): See Chapters 4 and 5.
  - Story
  - Discussion
- Do you prefer telling stories or having discussions? See Chapter 5.
- Do you understand the difference between a story and a personal essay? See Chapter 5.

## Paper 2 Checklist

- The name and correct spelling of the **title** and **author** of your **Single Text**. See Chapter 6.
- The **storyline** of your Single Text. You must know this in great detail. See Chapter 6.
- The main **characters** of your Single Text and their major **traits**. See Chapter 6.
- The **major themes** or issues raised by your Single Text. See Chapter 6.
- The names and correct spellings of the **texts** for your **Comparative Study**. See Chapter 7.
- Your favourite or 'anchor' text for the Comparative Study. Also, your least favourite, if you have studied three. See Chapter 7.
- The three **modes** for the Comparative Study. See Chapter 7.
- The **key moments** in your chosen Comparative Texts. See Chapter 7.
- The **terminology** associated with **poetry**. Most important: **imagery, poetic language** and **tone**. See Chapter 8.
- The value of understanding **feelings** in poetry and being able to write about them in your answers. See Chapter 8.

## General checklist

- The length of **time** that you can spend on each section of the exam. See the time guide above.
- The **length** that you expect your answers to be (in terms of pages or paragraphs).
- The importance of **structure** in your exam answers. Compositions will have defined features, as suggested in the questions. Paper 2 answers should follow the formula: **statement–quotation–comment**.
- **Spelling and mechanics** count for just **10 per cent** of all marks. See the marking scheme in Chapter 2.
- **60 per cent** of the marks is for **what** you write and **40 per cent** is for **how** you write it. See the marking scheme in Chapter 2.
- Remember: exam success is mostly about **preparation**, with a little **perspiration** some **inspiration** on the day!

If you are sure of all of the above, then you are well prepared for the Leaving Certificate English exam. However, a final word of warning: even the most seasoned English teacher will tell you that a certain amount of the exam is determined by the inspiration that a student experiences on the day. This cannot be taught. So, prepare well and do lots of work; then hope things go your way on the day!

Each student must do their very best with what they bring to the exam. The bottom line is to trust in your own ability. Generally, when you have worked really hard, you do reap rewards on the day of the exam.

Good luck!

# 10 Glossary of Useful Words

The words and phrases below appear throughout this book. Here's a reminder of their meaning.

**Aesthetics** are associated with beauty. Aesthetics are an essential aspect of creative writing.
**Alliteration** occurs when words that begin with the same letter are used close together for a sound effect.
**Anchor text**: This is the text that you know best from your Comparative Study. You will use this text as a base for your answers.
**Argumentative language** is logical language that aims to prove a point
**Atmosphere** is a word used to describe the feelings generated by a piece of writing or suggested by a picture.
**Audience**: Those who experience a text or drama; people who will read your written work.
**Bias** is the state of favouring one side or having a strong preference.
**Brainstorming** is the process of jotting down all of your thoughts related to a specific issue.
**Clarity** means being clear and certain in your writing.
**Cliché**: A tired, overused phrase that lacks originality.
**Climax** is the moment of highest tension in a text, film or drama.
**Coherence** means making logical sense from beginning to end.
**Commentary** is writing that comments on or gives an opinion about some other work. See the Examiner's Assessments on Sample Answers throughout the text.
**Composition**: This is the second section of Paper 1; a piece of written work composed by a writer.
**Comprehension** means 'understanding'. Also, it is the name of the first question on Paper 1. It tests your ability to respond to questions on a given text extract.
**Confidence** is the sum total of one's feeling about oneself. Having confidence means having belief in one's abilities.
**Diary**: A day-to-day, informal or personal account of events. It is usually in written form.
**Discussion**: To have a discussion means to talk about an issue, to declare an opinion and to share it. Discussion appears throughout the book.
**Emotive language** is language that gives rise to emotions and strong reactions.
**Format** means the form that a piece of writing takes, what it looks like and how it is structured. Examination of format appears throughout the book.
**Genre** means a type of work. Texts can be classified into different genres, e.g. comedy, tragedy, horror.
**Hero**: The main character in a text. Sometimes heroes have a fatal flaw or weakness (hubris) that brings about personal tragedy.
**Heroine**: This is a female hero.
**Hyperbole** is gross exaggeration or overstatement.
**Imagery** means pictures generated in the mind by the written word.
**Informative language** is language that gives factual information.
**Mechanics**: The mechanics of language include: spelling, grammar and punctuation. Mechanics are discussed throughout the book.
**Metaphor** is a colourful, creative description that is not to be understood literally. Metaphors are often found in poetry.

# GLOSSARY OF USEFUL WORDS

**Metre** is the beat or rhythm in a line of poetry.
**Modes of Comparison** are the headings under which you must compare texts in the Comparative Study.
**Mood** is the feeling generated by a text.
**Narrative language** is language used to tell a story.
**Objective**: An objective is something to aim for. 'Objective' has another meaning: to be objective means to be unbiased, to see things from all sides. The word 'objective' appears throughout the text.
**Onomatopoeia** occurs when the meaning of the word closely matches its sound, e.g. fizz, pop, crunch.
**Personification** occurs when non-human or inanimate objects are described as if they had human characteristics.
**Persuasive language** is language that tries to convince an audience of a particular viewpoint.
**Planning** is a vital aspect of writing any answer. Learn the art of being prepared! The notion of planning appears throughout the text.
**Pun**: This is a play on words. It occurs when words can be understood in more than one way.
**Purpose** is the reason behind something. You must always have a clear purpose when you are writing. Purpose appears throughout the book.
**Quotation**: The exact spoken words of a character in a text. Quotation appears throughout the text.
**Register** is a mixture of tone, vocabulary and purpose. Register is a vital characteristic that determines the success of your writing.
**Relationships** are an essential ingredient in all texts. Consider how people interact with each other in any text you study.
**Resolution** is the ending of a text.
**Rhetorical question**: This occurs when a question is asked and the answer is not given because it is either obvious or the questioner wants the audience to think and reflect.
**Rhyme** occurs when words that have similar sounds are used together for poetic effect.
**Sarcasm** is a scornful tone in writing and acting that pokes fun and can injure feelings.
**Simile** is a comparison that uses 'as' or 'like' to make a description more colourful.
**Slang** is low and somewhat vulgar forms of expression.
**Social setting** is the time and place in which a text is located.
**Stanza** is a collection of lines of poetry.
**Statement** is something written or spoken and usually presented as fact. Statements appear throughout the book.
**Structure** is how paragraphs and essays are shaped and put together. Structure is discussed throughout the book.
**Syntax** is the order in which words appear in a sentence.
**Tension** is a build-up of uncertainty, excitement or fear during a text.
**Theme** is the main issue raised or discussed by a text. It is more than just the plot or story.
**Tone** is the 'sound' of writing and the feeling suggested in its delivery. Tone creates a mood.
**Verbiage** is excessive language use, or writing that tries to sound sophisticated but isn't.
**Verbose**: To be verbose is to overuse language and sophisticated vocabulary that actually carries little genuine meaning.
**Villain**: the 'bad guy' in a text. Villains can be male or female.
**Visuals** are pictures, photographs, film stills, etc.
**Vocabulary** is a person's choice of words or level of language. Vocabulary is mentioned throughout the book.
**Waffle** is words that do not mean very much in the context of an exam answer.

## Acknowledgments

For permission to reproduce copyright material the publishers gratefully acknowledge the following:

'YouTube – Connecting Our World' by Gemma O'Doherty reprinted by kind permission of *The Irish Independent*. Extract from *The Kraken Wakes* by John Wyndham reprinted by kind permission of David Higham Associates. *A Removal from Terry Street* by Douglas Dunn reprinted by permission of United Agents on behalf of: Douglas Dunn. 'Seagull' by Brian McCabe from *Body Parts*, first published in Great Britain by Canongate Books Ltd, 14 High Street, Edinburgh, EH1 and reprinted with permission.

The publishers have made every effort to trace copyright holders, but if they have inadvertently overlooked any they will be pleased to make the necessary arrangements at the first opportunity.